Rethinking School Bullying

Routledge Research in Education

For a complete list of titles in this series, please visit www.routledge.com

60 **Picturebooks, Pedagogy and Philosophy**
   Joanna Haynes and Karin Murris

61 **Personal Epistemology and Teacher Education**
   Edited by Jo Brownlee, Gregory Schraw and Donna Berthelsen

62 **Teacher Learning that Matters**
   International Perspectives
   Edited by Mary Kooy and Klaas van Veen

63 **Pedagogy of Multiliteracies**
   Rewriting Goldilocks
   Heather Lotherington

64 **Intersectionality and "Race" in Education**
   Edited by Kalwant Bhopal and John Preston

65 **The Politics of Education**
   Challenging Multiculturalism
   Edited by Christos Kassimeris and Marios Vryonides

66 **Whiteness and Teacher Education**
   Edie White

67 **Multidisciplinary Approaches to Educational Research**
   Case Studies from Europe and the Developing World
   Edited by Sadaf Rizvi

68 **Postcolonial Perspectives on Global Citizenship Education**
   Edited by Vanessa de Oliveira Andreotti and Lynn Mario T. M. De Souza

69 **Education in the Black Diaspora**
   Perspectives, Challenges, and Prospects
   Edited by Kassie Freeman and Ethan Johnson

70 **Gender, Race, and the Politics of Role Modelling**
   The Influence of Male Teachers
   Wayne Martino and Goli Rezai-Rashti

71 **Educating for Diversity and Social Justice**
   Amanda Keddie

72 **Considering Trilingual Education**
   Kathryn Henn-Reinke

73 **Commitment, Character, and Citizenship**
   Religious Education in Liberal Democracy
   Edited by Hanan A. Alexander and Ayman K. Agbaria

74 **Adolescent Literacies in a Multicultural Context**
   Edited by Alister Cumming

75 **Participation, Facilitation, and Mediation**
Children and Young People in Their Social Contexts
Edited by Claudio Baraldi and Vittorio Iervese

76 **The Politics of Knowledge in Education**
Elizabeth Rata

77 **Neoliberalism, Pedagogy and Human Development**
Exploring Time, Mediation and Collectivity in Contemporary Schools
Michalis Kontopodis

78 **Resourcing Early Learners**
New Networks, New Actors
Sue Nichols, Jennifer Rowsell, Helen Nixon and Sophia Rainbird

79 **Educating for Peace in a Time of "Permanent War"**
Are Schools Part of the Solution or the Problem?
Edited by Paul R. Carr and Brad J. Porfilio

80 **The Politics of Teacher Professional Development**
Policy, Research and Practice
Ian Hardy

81 **Working-Class Minority Students' Routes to Higher Education**
Roberta Espinoza

82 **Education, Indigenous Knowledges, and Development in the Global South**
Contesting Knowledges for a Sustainable Future
Anders Breidlid

83 **Teacher Development in Higher Education**
Existing Programs, Program Impact, and Future Trends
Edited by Eszter Simon and Gabriela Pleschová

84 **Virtual Literacies**
Interactive Spaces for Children and Young People
Edited by Guy Merchant, Julia Gillen, Jackie Marsh and Julia Davies

85 **Geography and Social Justice in the Classroom**
Edited by Todd W. Kenreich

86 **Diversity, Intercultural Encounters, and Education**
Edited by Susana Gonçalves and Markus A. Carpenter

87 **The Role of Participants in Education Research**
Ethics, Epistemologies, and Methods
Edited by Warren Midgley, Patrick Alan Danaher and Margaret Baguley

88 **Care in Education**
Teaching with Understanding and Compassion
Sandra Wilde

89 **Family, Community, and Higher Education**
Edited by Toby S. Jenkins

90 **Rethinking School Bullying**
Dominance, Identity and School Culture
Ronald B. Jacobson

Rethinking School Bullying
Dominance, Identity and School Culture

Ronald B. Jacobson

NEW YORK AND LONDON

First published 2013
by Routledge
711 Third Avenue, New York, NY 10017

Simultaneously published in the UK
by Routledge
2 Park Square, Milton Park, Abingdon, Oxfordshire OX14 4RN

First issued in paperback 2014

*Routledge is an imprint of the Taylor & Francis Group,
an informa business*

© 2013 Taylor & Francis

The right of Ronald B. Jacobson to be identified as author of this work has been asserted in accordance with sections 77 and 78 of the Copyright, Designs and Patents Act 1988.

All rights reserved. No part of this book may be reprinted or reproduced or utilised in any form or by any electronic, mechanical, or other means, now known or hereafter invented, including photocopying and recording, or in any information storage or retrieval system, without permission in writing from the publishers.

Trademark Notice: Product or corporate names may be trademarks or registered trademarks, and are used only for identification and explanation without intent to infringe.

Library of Congress Cataloging-in-Publication Data
Jacobson, Ronald B.
  Rethinking school bullying : dominance, identity and school culture / Ronald B. Jacobson.
    p. cm. — (Routledge research in education ; 90)
  Includes bibliographical references and index.
 1. Bullying in schools. 2. Bullying—Prevention. 3. School children—Conduct of life. 4. School environment—United States. I. Title.
  LB3013.3.J3 2012
  371.5'8—dc23
  2012031137

ISBN 13: 978-0-415-63626-1 (hbk)
ISBN 13: 978-1-138-83392-0 (pbk)

Typeset in Sabon
by IBT Global.

To Michele, Katie & Andrew—I am indebted to the years of conversation with you that have shaped so much of my thinking.

Contents

1	The Southside Bump Game: An Introduction	1
2	Bullying Research: What Bullying Looks Like and Where It Comes From	10
3	Current Anti-Bullying Work: A Fly in the Ointment	41
4	Student Identity Construction: Rethinking the Dominance of Bullying	45
5	Dominance and Schooling: Parallel Narratives from the Same Cloth	60
6	Need, Stories, and Moral Life: Behavior Comes from Somewhere	73
7	Re-Storying a School: Resistance, Taxonomy, and Kindergarten	84
8	Toward a Holistic Anti-Bullying Model: Culture, Safety, and Moral Transformation	101
	Notes	147
	References	153
	Index	161

1 The Southside Bump Game
An Introduction

> By kindergarten, however, a structure begins to be revealed and will soon be carved in stone. Certain children will have the right to limit the social experiences of their classmates. Henceforth a ruling class will notify others of their acceptability, and the outsiders learn to anticipate the sting of rejection. Long after hitting and name-calling have been outlawed by the teachers, a more damaging phenomenon is allowed to take root, spreading like a weed from grade to grade. Must it be so? (Paley 1992, 3)

I begin this discussion with a vignette based upon an incident that occurred among sixth-graders. I interject this story not as a case study or as a site of analysis, but, instead, as an illustrative example of school bullying. In a sense, the story allows me to "flesh out" what bullying looks like on the playground as well as the typical anti-bullying responses employed by schools. The telling of the *Southside Incident*, as I will call it, involves the use of a composite story,[1] setting up the key ideas outlined in the empirical research which will provide focal points for our discussion. I begin, then, with the story of a trio of boys, a game of "bump" and a passive sixth-grader who learned to anticipate the sting of rejection.

THE SOUTHSIDE INCIDENT

The birthday party had been anticipated for weeks. A number of boys from Southside had made the invitation list to the overnight affair and felt privileged to be there. It was always a social coup to be noticed by Jake, and even more so to be invited to one of his functions. Yet, Sammy and Jeff knew they would be on the list. The trio (Jake, Sammy and Jeff) had a long history together and another birthday party simply cemented their camaraderie. Matthew had been invited this year as well. A snapshot taken that evening captures all four boys at the party. Jake, front and center is seated behind his new drum set, clowning, filling the picture with his persona. Sammy and Jeff are together on one side of the drum set with their eyes fastened on Jake, laughing uproariously at his antics. Matthew is on the other side of the set, distracted from the boys by the camera, shyly smiling, holding one of Jake's extra drumsticks. The picture tells a story in and of itself, but who were these boys that became so tangled that sixth-grade year?

Jake, Sammy, and Jeff

Jake, Sammy, Jeff, and Matthew had attended Southside K-8 since kindergarten. Jake was definitely the leading force within the group of four. He was popular—perhaps one of the most popular students at Southside. Jake was athletic, musical, a good student and came from a solidly middle-class family. Jake was a kid that many gravitated toward, a student that everyone wanted to know, an individual whose acceptance marked something important. He and Matthew had forged a relationship over the course of the years. I would not call it a friendship, but Matthew hoped that it might become one. Matthew, beyond being invited to the birthday party, had spent time in Jake's home on several occasions. Similarly, Jake had also spent time in Matthew's house on an occasional weekend. They enjoyed each other's company. Jake's older siblings, having attended Southside, were now at the local high school excelling in a number of ways. Jake's parents expected him, like his siblings, to rise above the crowd. He had a reputation to live up to and they were always quick to remind him of that fact. On the basketball floor Jake was compelled to either be the star or the clown. As a member of the school math team, he was expected to win top honors. On the soccer field, where he excelled—typically scoring more goals than his teammates—the watching eyes of his family expected him to save the game from defeat. Yet, his prowess—even at soccer—still paled in light of his older brothers' high school football careers. His parents, strict and often demanding, expected great things from him. The pressure was significant. His public image—especially with adults—was important. Jake, thus, became an expert at putting his best foot forward with those who had the power to reward or affirm. Jake, though popular, had a lot to live up to.

Sammy, less popular at Southside, lived in Jake's shadow. He was insecure and aggressive—enjoying rough and tumble physical play; he was also quick to get angry. He struggled academically. He was involved in sports, yet lacked any exceptional athletic skills. He too had forged a somewhat distant relationship with Matthew. They both, in fact all four boys, played on the same basketball and soccer teams. Sammy had spent time in Matthew's house at sleepovers and birthday parties. Matthew had been invited to dinner with Sammy's family on several occasions. Though Matthew's relationship with Sammy would, again, not be characterized by the word friendship, the two had enjoyed playing together. While certainly friendship with Jake was the prize everyone sought, hanging out with Sammy was something Matthew enjoyed. Sammy's parents were also demanding, expecting him to excel. He was often grounded and privileges were withheld because of a less than satisfactory report card. Though Sammy could be characterized as aggressive, his younger brother, Taylor, was even more so (e.g. belittling his classmates, physically fighting with others). Taylor excelled athletically and maintained solid grades. Sammy's parents typically expected more from Sammy than from Taylor because "he was the oldest." Sammy's grades and athletic abilities (important currency in his family) paled next to Taylor's. Sammy's parents bullied him toward better grades; threatening, punishing, and disparaging him. Taylor's success, overtly held before Sammy by his parents, furthered Sammy's own sense of inadequacy.

Jeff was an only child. Though sensitive (he could be brought to tears), he carefully hid such "weaknesses" from others. Jeff was the one of this group of three that Matthew might consider a real friend. They slept over at each other's houses, went to baseball games together, and enjoyed the same hobbies. One such hobby was collecting small figurines from the local toy store. These figurines came in shades of black or grey, and part of the fun of collecting was painting them. Of course both Matthew and Jeff envied the painting skills of those who worked at the local hobby store, whose figurines were displayed in the window. Both boys spent hours perfecting their craft. When they would paint together, Jeff would insist on painting certain aspects of Matthew's figurines (because, as he would confidently boast, "I can paint the details better"). Matthew, not wanting to make a scene, would acquiesce. In spite of this Matthew still enjoyed being with Jeff; playing imagination games, acting out battle scenes, wandering the mall in search of the perfect figurine. Jeff's parents, caring deeply for Jeff, often treated him with indulgence; they found a way to give him what he asked for, they required little from him and they were permissive with his behavior. "Boys will be boys," was their motto. Jeff, though, struggled in several ways important to others. Although he was on the same sports teams as the boys, he was always a step behind. He also consistently lagged academically. Further, Jeff was sensitive, making rejection intensely painful. But, that sensitivity was masked by male bravado and a devil-may-care attitude. Jeff longed to fit in and sought attention in a number of ways. Ultimately, Jeff sought Jake's attention. He desired to be Jake's right-hand man; one who Jake chose, one in who Jake confided. Matthew, though at times fun to play with, simply paled in Jeff's eyes when it came to what Jake could offer. Matthew was not popular enough to give Jeff what he sought.

Matthew

In an old classroom photograph taken during his sixth-grade year Matthew is larger than life. As Matthew is acting the clown in the photograph, one notices both his joy and his longing to fit in—to find acceptance. His arms are stretched wide across the picture partially hiding two classmates next to him in this classroom snapshot (probably taken by a parent). The classmates captured in the picture are laughing, obviously finding this bit of Matthew-bravado amusing. This picture was taken at the beginning of Matthew's sixth-grade year.

Matthew was passionate both in his sense of justice (e.g. becoming indignant when another was treated unfairly) and in his convictions (some might say he was stubborn, or perhaps simply persistent). Matthew was often drawn to kids who were outside of the popular circles at school. It was not that Matthew had a dream of pulling outsiders into the greater community of friendship within the school. Instead, Matthew simply enjoyed being with all kinds of people, and though he was very aware of the popular/unpopular landscape, those lines of demarcation meant little to him when it came to choosing friends or project partners. So, while Matthew at times hung out with the "right" crowd, he just as often found himself with a less than popular student.

Although Matthew was not afraid to state his opinion, he disliked making waves. When aggressed upon personally Matthew was much more likely to quietly walk away rather than fight back. Some might find this way passive, but perhaps pacifist would be a better term. Matthew would stick up for others, but often declined to be forceful when he was targeted. This propensity becomes important to the story I am telling, along with one other dangerous trait; Matthew could be brought to tears. While he often would not fight back physically or verbally, his sensitive nature allowed the impact of those interactions to mark him deeply on an emotional level. Matthew did not cry on a daily basis, really not that often at all, but in the world of developing adolescent masculine egos within the sixth-grade milieu that was Southside K-8 one male tear was too many. Yet, Matthew had flourished at Southside for six years. Here Matthew received adequate grades, was an average athlete, played in the band, and had cultivated a number of friendships.

Jake, Sammy, Jeff, and Matthew were ordinary kids who attended a good school, a school where kids were cared for and attended to by parents and teachers alike. In many ways Jake, Sammy, Jeff, and Matthew were content Southsiders, enmeshed in the culture of the only school they had known. Life shifted for them during the course of their sixth-grade year as the result of a playground game called *bump*.

A Game of Bump

Bump is a typical recess game played with a couple basketballs, a hoop, and a number of kids all vying to knock each other out. The game is simple. The players line up single file at the free throw line. The first two participants have basketballs. The first person in line shoots at the basket. If the player makes the shot, he or she collects the ball and passes it to the next person in line without a ball. If the shot is missed, then the next player in line is freed to shoot as well. If the player behind the initial shooter makes a basket first, then the initial shooter is relegated to the sidelines. The game is fast paced and continues until only one player is left; the winner. Bump was, in a sense, a status symbol at Southside. The 'who's who' of intermediate recess lined up each afternoon while the rest of the school envyingly eyed the spectacle. At a typical recess from twenty to thirty children were involved in the bump game. Early in Matthew's sixth-grade year a group of boys began to target him in this members-only recess game. Jake, Sammy, and Jeff made a pact. They determined to purposely miss shots to keep each other in (this part of the plan was not all that unusual; everyone wanted to stay in the game and hoping one's friends would remain engaged until the end was a common desire among participants). But, also in the plan, was a decision to always try to knock Matthew out first. The ploy began with three boys, in the midst of twenty to thirty other children, seeking to eliminate one boy first. Matthew was frustrated by their targeting, but the impact of the scheme was mitigated by the sheer number of people involved.

But this targeting took a turn. This group of three boys began to recruit others in the bump game to join in until the impetus of the entire game became focused on knocking Matthew out first. Matthew continued to play because of his desire to fit in, but after being knocked out first each day he would walk away in tears as the crowd of twenty to thirty peers would roar with triumphant laughter, proclaiming their approval at his elimination. Jake, Sammy, and Jeff became celebrities within the group. Classmates would smile knowingly at Jake as the bump game began (anticipating the "real game" focused on eliminating Matthew), and then pat him (Jake) on the back as Matthew would be relegated to the sideline each day. Sammy and Jeff were also smiled at and congratulated for their role in this humiliating ploy. Matthew, on the other hand, was left confused. Angry, hurt, isolated; but most of all, confused. What had he done to cause this, or, better, to deserve this? Why had these three boys decided to target him? Why had they inflamed the entire bump crowd against him and, further, why would these other classmates follow Jake's leading? For him, this was beyond comprehension. He certainly would have stood up for one being targeted so viciously. Foundationally, his confusion was expressed in the obvious question: how could he make it stop?

Beyond the Bump Game

The bullying of Matthew masterminded by Jake, Sammy, and Jeff began with the bump game, but played out in other ways. This exclusion soon moved beyond the bump game to other parts of his day, including his life away from school. He was shunned during class group projects, he was no longer invited to birthday parties, he was "accidentally" tripped at soccer practice, he began to eat lunch alone. The bullying of Matthew became pervasive. It was overt: he was laughed at, he was tripped in the hallway, his books were stolen from his desk then hidden (to the delight of those watching), etc. It was covert: he was excluded from group social activities, he was confronted by the whispering of others and knowing eyes that mocked him, rumors were started about him regarding his home life and his personal habits, etc. And, it was relational: the trio encouraged others to target Matthew, his friends no longer talked with him (he was off limits), etc. Though he did not understand why, Matthew had become a pariah, the one chosen to not belong, the one deemed—first by a small group of peers, then by the larger class—to be unworthy of friendship. Early, after the bump game turned sour, these three boys would periodically continue to let Matthew into their circle. But that circle had changed significantly. Whenever all three (Jake, Sammy, and Jeff) were together, the relations were devious and Matthew recognized this. For example, that spring all four boys attended a local concert put on by the school. Matthew approached the trio and talked for awhile. Then Sammy whispered something to Jake and Jeff, prompting the three to run away from Matthew. Matthew followed, again not understanding the game into which he was being drawn. The trio would slow until Matthew would nearly catch up. Then, on the verge of being caught, they would laugh and run away again only to repeat the scene. Now many would question why Matthew did not just walk away. Eventually he did, but there still lived in him the hope that these "friends" would accept him back into the fold. This circle of friendship had been altered significantly and Matthew sought to bring it back into conformity with earlier days.

When Matthew encountered the boys separately a variety of differing interactions would transpire. Jeff would converse with Matthew, but always with a tone of belligerence hidden just under the surface. Sammy maintained a similar stance. He was somewhat cordial to Matthew one-on-one, but with a palpable air of contempt and disdain toward him. Interestingly, Sammy's younger brother would rail verbal abuse at Matthew from the sidelines at soccer practice.[2] Jake's one-on-one relationship with Matthew was perhaps the most perplexing. When alone with Matthew, Jake would express kindness, interest, and civility. Matthew would often leave those conversations thinking, perhaps, that Jake had decided to be his friend again; perhaps the nightmare was over. But always, when with the group, Jake would reject Matthew, often hiding behind the more overt verbal abuse delivered by Sammy and Jeff. In some ways it seemed that Jake ran the show, but did not want to get his hands dirty. He had Sammy and Jeff do the messy work of bullying Matthew.

Matthew assumed the position all hoped to avoid, that of outcast. He was lost, the scapegoat. He had become the target of boys he thought and hoped were friends. Beyond that, a number of students within the larger student body joined in. He had been rejected by students that he did not even know. He endured school, anticipating the last bell of the day not simply to go home and play, but to escape the heartache that the school day had become. It was not until mid-winter that Matthew informed his family of the situation. After informing his parents, each day he would arrive home in tears spending the evenings in long conversations with his family about the pain of what was happening, looking for strategies to end the abuse. Over the course of that year Matthew moved from the larger than life snapshot taken of him in September to a much more passive, afraid, and hopeless eleven-year-old. His grades fell, his significant friends became his parents and sister, he became much more cynical and negative about the world (school in particular), and he became hyper-critical of himself. He had come to believe that he was the problem, that he was unlikable, that he had nothing to offer. At times Matthew despaired of life.

School Response

As indicated above, it was not until well after winter break that Matthew's parents came to understand the situation. Matthew had been more sullen that fall, but he had been unwilling to offer any information regarding what had been happening at school. Matthew was both ashamed to talk about the situation and was afraid parent involvement might simply make things worse. Finally, after the weight had become unbearable, Matthew confided in his parents. Even after this, though, Matthew strongly protested any thought of his parents contacting the school or the bullies' parents. Instead solutions focused on "Matthew-based" strategies: avoiding the perpetrators, standing up for himself, and patiently waiting, hoping this aberration would pass. Finally, as winter wore on, Matthew relented and allowed his parents to notify the school administration regarding the situation.

The school was quick to respond. The bullies were summoned to the office and certain anti-bullying activities began. First, a campaign aimed at raising awareness was begun. The bullies were required to read the sections of the school handbook pertaining to respect, relational interaction, and bullying activities. Definitions of bullying were outlined for them, as were school policy and expectations. The bullies also underwent what one might call "empathy" training. The ramifications of their actions in Matthew's life were explained. Role-playing activities meant to foster perspective taking were enacted aimed at increasing understanding and empathy in the bullies. These awareness-raising activities were also directed toward the school at large. Assemblies were held on the topic of bullying (defining it, articulating school policy, encouraging peer pressure and response aimed at eradicating it). Banners and posters were put up around the school addressing notions of respect, acceptance, and care. Parents and families were also informed of school policy and expectations.

Second, programs of skill-based training were set in motion. Jake and the trio underwent aggression management training, empathy development training, and social skills training. They were taught appropriate uses and places for aggression. They were taught ways to mitigate anger in more appropriate ways. They were trained to gain status through more appropriate avenues (e.g., grades or on the sports field). They were trained to see life from the point of view of others; to better understand the feelings or experiences of others. They were taught to read social cues more accurately and to relate in a more caring manner.

Third, regimes of disciplinary training were enacted. The bullies were reprimanded. Certain punitive actions were meted out (e.g., detentions, loss of recess privileges). Rewards for non-bullying actions as well as consequences for future bullying activities were clearly articulated. The parents of the bullies were informed of their child's activities, hoping that these parents would bring disciplinary and rehabilitative actions to bear in the home. The bullies were, then, watched in the classroom and on the playground, making sure that they were compliant with school bullying policy and rules. When being informed, or trained, or reprimanded by the administration Jake would respond politely, Sammy would smirk, and Jeff would cower. In the presence of adults all three would agree to stop their actions toward Matthew, but outside the purview of the administration they would laugh and joke about the situation, blowing it off as yet another example of a school principal with nothing better to do.

Matthew, on the other hand, was protected. Teachers were asked to monitor him and his interactions throughout the day. Attempts were also made to bolster his confidence and aggressiveness (i.e. exhorting him not to cry in public, encouraging him to take a more aggressive stance toward confrontation, helping him to find ways to "blow off" hurtful remarks). Yet, Matthew in some ways now had moved even further from his peers as the administration and teachers rallied around him. The adults had come to the rescue. Matthew had to be protected by them while they punished Jake, Sammy, and Jeff on his behalf.

Unfortunately, despite the administration's best intentions, the bullying continued. Jake, Sammy, Jeff, and a host of others continued to exclude and target Matthew. Admittedly the bullying was better conceived, more covert, but not any less viscous. Though all looked well on the outside (e.g. the bump game, after it was reinstated, looked much more fair), Matthew knew that all was not well (e.g. rather than heaping abuse on him during the bump game, everyone simply ignored him). He began to live a life of non-existence and subtle abuse. He came to the conclusion that the bullying he continued to experience could not be fixed by well-meaning teachers, administrators, or even parents.

Beginning Again, Remaining the Same

Southside was a K-8 school, meaning that graduation from sixth grade, while involving a transition to middle school, was not a transition to a new school-house. Most within Southside continued to seventh grade in the same building, with the same group of friends and the same familiarity with staff and routines. Matthew, though, after agonizing over the decision, chose to transfer to the Uptown Middle School across town to begin seventh grade. He knew no one at Uptown. It took most of his seventh grade year to decide, but by the end of that year Matthew believed he had made the right choice. Since then Matthew has moved on to the local high school, maintaining solid friendships, with no signs of the bullying he experienced at Southside. But, the scars of that sixth-grade year continue to mark Matthew's life. He is more cynical; more reserved, and certainly has shrunk from the bravado of that sixth-grade snapshot. He is also much more careful with his tears or any kind of emotionality. He has learned that emotions are best hidden from peers.

Jake, Sammy, and Jeff continued on at Southside their seventh grade year. Matthew was forgotten. But, they soon began to target another boy. Trent was a bit of an outsider, struggled socially, and could have an explosive temper. He became the new pariah and the new target for Jake, Sammy, and Jeff. They, again, were reprimanded and watched. Trent was trained to have better social skills. The bullying continued until all moved on to high school. At that point I lost track of Jake and his friends.

Southside, like so many schools, continues to fight the daily battle against bullying within its walls. This battle is waged through special anti-bullying assembly speakers, structured empathy building encounters, bullying awareness campaigns, anti-bullying training programs, programs fostering skill development (anger management, social skills development), clearly articulated and posted rules and procedures regarding bullying (complete with rewards for compliance and consequences for non-compliance) and concerted whole-school (recruiting students, teachers and adult volunteers) monitoring and surveillance. Despite these programs, as Paley articulates, certain children persistently work to "limit the social experiences of their classmates. . . . A ruling class [continues to] notify others of their acceptability, and the outsiders learn to anticipate the sting of rejection" (1992, 3). Toward the end of Matthew's sixth-grade year, Jeff was asked why it was that he had targeted Matthew. After a bit of thought, Jeff matter-of-factly replied, "because I like to make him cry."

CONCLUSION

This project, while neither purporting to be the last word on school bullying nor claiming to be the first word by negating important empirical conceptions, offers an expanded word. It raises a number of key questions that are important both to our understanding of, as well as our strategies aimed against bullying. Jake was reprimanded, he was taught not to bully, he was trained to wield new non-aggressive skills, he was made aware of Matthew's feelings, and he was watched. But the bullying of Matthew continued. What leads one child to bully another? Why does a ruling class develop within schools, a group of students who notify others of their acceptability? What realities inform, motivate, and guide such activities? These questions become critical in understanding why educators could not stop the bullying of Matthew. Further, these questions open a window into an important aspect of our self-understanding as human beings. This book, while considering school bullying, fundamentally explores the satisfaction humans derive in the tears of another and re-imagines what it means to be human together. I turn, now, to the empirical literature on school bullying.

2 Bullying Research
What Bullying Looks Like and Where It Comes From

> Columbine changed how our society views school violence. . . . Columbine offered an opportunity to open our nation's eyes to the pain so many of our kids feel as they confront emotional violence at school. . . . The school shooters acted in a terrible way and with a sense of outrage and even justification that many kids around America felt—and feel. These students believe that they have to endure a school dominated by emotional violence that no one, specifically no adult, will do anything about it. In that belief they represent an extreme form of a common, shared experience. What is that common experience? It is the experience of bullying—as a perpetrator, a victim, or a bystander. Like sexual abuse, bullying is a core issue in the development and behavior of American kids. It is linked to the quality of their emotional lives and has far-reaching implications for their academic development, their relationships with adults and peers, and their sense of peace and well-being. (Garbarino 2004, xi–xii)

THE PHENOMENON OF SCHOOL BULLYING

A bump game gone bad. Three sixth-grade boys conspire to target a classmate. Twenty to thirty students join in, roaring their approval at the humiliation of another. A young sixth-grader is forced to transfer to a new school at the hands of a few. The next year, a new target. And why? "Because," proclaims one perpetrator, "I like to make him cry."

The bump game became the site of an initial foray into what the literature calls a bullying encounter. In this chapter I offer a brief overview of how current research conceptualizes bullying relations, the processes that bring them about, the characters that both form and are formed in such encounters and the strategies aimed at ending the domination of bullying on the playground. I begin by outlining the strategies aimed at assessing the phenomenon within schooling.

Assessment

Gaining accurate information on the extent and nature of the bullying relationship is difficult for several reasons. First, bullying often takes place covertly, with bullies knowing that it is "against the rules." This, then, makes outside observation, though important, incomplete. For example, it often becomes difficult for a teacher or a parent to distinguish between friendship and abuse on the playground. Bullying can be a subtle look, a whispered word, a covert exclusion, or an "accidental" bump in the hallway between classes—all of which could be shared between the best of friends or become the subtle tools of humiliation directed toward a classmate.

Assessing the atmosphere of bullying within a school also becomes difficult because students are reluctant to talk about it, to self-disclose. The reasons are obvious for the bully (i.e., not wanting to get in trouble). But, even for the victim, admission to being bullied can often be seen as an admission of failure. Asking a teacher or parent for help may simply invite more bullying, granted more carefully hidden and cunningly wrought, but most students believe teachers and parents can do little to help (Simmons, 2002). Another reason that assessment becomes difficult is simply because only the bully and the bullied know the nuances of their experience. Their perceptions, while real, are influenced by a number of factors making clear assessment tenuous. Furlong et al. underline this issue:

> Ultimately, only the bully knows his or her motivation (although they may have rationalized it in a self-supporting manner) and the victim only knows if she or he experienced harm (although even here there may be some forms of denial or self-protective reframing of the experience). On the other hand, bullies and victims may not be the best judges of the motivation of their behavior and the interpretation of the emotional reactions. (2003, 468)

With such obstacles, a number of bullying assessment tools have been developed over the past thirty years. They fall into several broad categories. First, researchers often use self-reporting instruments, such as surveys, to gather data on bullying. The major tool used by Dan Olweus, who is considered by many to be the pioneer of modern bullying research, is a questionnaire handed out to students asking them of their personal experiences with bullying over time (1993). Self-reports, in various forms, essentially ask students (assuring confidentiality) how often they have engaged in certain behaviors over a certain period of time. This kind of self-reporting garners information on those who victimize as well as those who are victimized. Self-reporting data can also be collected from parents, teachers, etc. regarding their perceptions of school climate, bullying activity, as well as the family dynamics of students within the school.

Peer nomination is another prevalent tool in assessing bullying. Essentially peer nomination involves interviewing or surveying students at large about their classmates. A list of classmates may be given to a student, who is asked to separate names according to certain criteria (e.g., students who bully, students who get bullied, etc.). A third assessment method involves behavioral observations. "For example, Craig and Pepler videotaped aggressive and socially competent Canadian children in Grades 1 through 6 on the playground [finding that] peers were involved in bullying in an astounding 85% of bully episodes" (Espelage and Swearer 2003, 370). Through this videotaping, researchers have been able to break down specific types of bullying involvement by peers (e.g., onlooker, co-perpetrator, watcher, or interceder) in the bullying encounter.

Using such assessment tools are helpful in understanding the prevalence of bullying within a school, attitudes toward such activities held by both adults and students, as well as pointing out which students regularly bully and are bullied. But, the complicity of school, culture, family, peer groups, and individual student characteristics deepen the complexity of bullying, making any assessment difficult and complex. There are a number of reasons why students hesitate to implicate themselves or their classmates in bullying activity, making bullying assessment within a classroom or on the playground an incomplete science.

Definitions

Jake, Sammy, and Jeff decided to "have a little fun" with Matthew. They conspired with others to knock him out of a recess game first. They laughed, along with the crowd, at his humiliation. He was excluded from their circle of friendship by means of "knowing whispers", sly smiles, subtle bumps in the hallway, as well as overt rejections and harsh words. These interactions continued over the course of several months and only ceased when Matthew left the school. At least one of the perpetrators did all of this because he enjoyed the tears of Matthew. Matthew's grades plummeted, his self-regard was greatly lowered—he became much less confident and unsure of himself, and he often despaired of attending school and, at times, of life itself. But, was the Southside Incident a bullying encounter and, if so, why?

Research has, indeed, carefully and methodically sought to lay out definitional/descriptive parameters surrounding bullying. The Scottish Council for Research in Education defines bullying, "as a willful, conscious desire to hurt or threaten or frighten someone else" (Johnson, Munn, and Edwards 1991). Fabre-Cornali, Emin, and Pain—French researchers—contend that bullying includes "crime and offences against people or against personal or school property . . . which disturb school life" (1999, 130). Frey and Hoppe-Graff, studying Brazilian preschool children, describe bullying as "dominant aggression which occurs when an unprovoked child taunts, intimidates, coerces, makes fun of or assaults another child—without a clear external goal for this behaviour" (1994, 250). Dan Olweus asserts that "a student is being bullied or victimized when he or she is exposed, repeatedly and over time to negative actions on the part of one or more other students (1993, 9). "It must be stressed," Olweus continues, that the term bullying is not (or should not be) used when two students of approximately the same strength (physical or psychological) are fighting or quarreling. In order to use the term bullying, there should be an imbalance in strength (an asymmetric power relationship): The student who is exposed to the negative actions has difficulty defending him/herself and is somewhat helpless against the student or students who harass. (1993, 10)

While bullying is defined with varying nuances within the literature (Roland 1989, 143; Naylor and Cowie 1999, 467; Furlong et al 2003, 467; Holt and Keys 2004, 121; Atlas and Pepler 1998, 87), Horne et al. assert that "there are three common components to all definitions of bullying. First, it is a purposeful aggressive behavior [i.e., it is not accidental]. Second, there is an imbalance of power between the victim and the bully. Third, it occurs more than once. It is important," Horne et al. continue, "that teachers, students, and parents understand how bullying is different from play and recognize it for what it is—an abuse of power. Bullying behaviors are instrumental, that is, they serve to achieve a goal" (2004, 298). Salmivalli and Neiminen concur arguing that "school bullying is typically defined as deliberate and systematic negative actions repeatedly targeted at one and the same victim who is relatively defenseless in front of the perpetrator(s)" (2002, 32).

Specifically, how might we understand the aggressive or "negative" actions involved in bullying?[1] These "negative actions," Olweus explains,

> can be carried out by words (verbally), for instance, by threatening, taunting, teasing, and calling names. It is a negative action when some boy hits, pushes, kicks, pinches, or restrains another—by physical contact. It is also possible to carry out negative actions without use of words or physical contact, such as by making faces or dirty gestures, intentionally excluding someone from a group, or refusing to comply with another person's wishes. (1993, 9)

Furlong et al. contend that for behavior to be considered bullying "the behavior may need to disrupt learning or the school environment, cause emotional stress or distress in a victim, or result in physical harm to a student (2003, 457). Pellegrini and Long differentiate bullying aggression from reactive aggression:

> Bullying, for us, is a specific form of aggression and one that is used deliberately to secure resources. In this regard it is a dimension of proactive aggression and distinct from aggression which is used relatively, or aggression which is used in response to social provocation. (2004, 108)

Put simply, reactive aggression involves response to some stimulus. We might envision Matthew lashing out at Jake or Jeff or Sammy in response to their exclusion of him. On the other hand, proactive aggression, rather than being a reaction to the aggression of others, is instrumental action focused on rewards. Salmivalli and Nieminen further delineate proactive aggression by what they call,

> instrumental aggression and bullying, the former referring to behavior in which aggression is used as a means to get an external reward, such as when a child pushes another to take a toy from him/her, the latter to person-directed, "mean" aggression in which no such goal is necessarily detected.[2] (2002, 32)

In terms of the proactive aggression involved in the bullying dynamic, the literature distinguishes between two or three nuances of expression: direct or overt aggression, indirect or covert aggression, as well as social or relational aggression. By direct aggression we imagine physical fighting (e.g. hitting, pushing, tripping, slapping) or verbal abuse (e.g. teasing, name-calling) (Espelage and Swearer, 2003; Olweus, 1993; Juvonen and Graham, 2001). By indirect aggression we imagine interactions that often travel through a third party (e.g. rumor spreading) and can include exclusion, whispering, and silences (Olweus, 1993; Simmons 2002; Juvonen and Graham, 2001). Finally, social or relational aggression points toward the use of relationships to harm another or of intentional effort toward harming the relationships of another (Simmons, 2002; Brown, 2003; Espelage and Swearer, 2004). Kaukianen et al. see social or relational aggression as a component of indirect aggression (1999, 83). In fact, they side with additional research that breaks aggression into a developmental tripartite: physical aggression (more prevalent in young children), verbal aggression (at the arrival of sufficient verbal skills), and indirect aggression (surfacing later as the more sophisticated social skills of manipulation develop) (1999, 84). In considering the nuances between direct, indirect, and social or relational aggression one is struck with their overlap. Here my attempt is not to build walls between different forms of aggression, but to highlight the nuances of power abuse and the intentional harm evident in various avenues of bullying. The borders between direct, indirect, and social bullying are often fuzzy, but the effects of each are devastating.

Bullying, then, is proactive, it is repeated over time, it is targeted upon a victim, and it may involve verbal abuse, physical abuse, or subtle relational disruption. It is disruptive to the learning environment and to the victim's well-being and involves elements of asymmetric power focused on securing some objective (whether tangible—e.g., lunch money; or intangible—e.g., social status). Bullying is also dyadic (between individuals—Jake and Matthew; Jeff and Matthew; Sammy and Matthew) and it is enmeshed in peer relations (e.g., the dynamics of the bump game). Such bullying continues to be a pervasive feature of the school landscape. Indeed, on this definition, the activities on that Southside playground are a clear example of bullying.

Pervasiveness

In his research of bullying in Norway and Sweden in the early 1980s, Olweus found that one in seven, or 15% %of all students in primary and junior high schools, had been involved in bullying (as a bully or victim) "now and then" or more frequently (1993). He reported that 9%%, or 52,000 of those surveyed were victims, while 7%%, or 41,000 bullied others with some consistency. Nine thousand, or 1.6%%, were classified as bully/victims (students who both bullied and were victims of bullying) (1993). Boivin et al. concur with this finding, asserting that between 13 and 16%% of students are rejected by their peers. Repeated rejection, according to Boivin et al., is experienced by a somewhat smaller population (2001).

> Research on bully/victim problems indicates that approximately 10% of children in elementary and middle schools are repeatedly harassed and victimized by schoolmates. Studies also show that victimization tends to be rather stable over time, with the same children enduring these negative peer experiences year after year. (2001, 266)

Research by Craig et al. that focused on Canadian children found a slightly higher bullying involvement.

> Research in Canada and other countries indicates that the %age of children who report victimization (20%) is higher than the %age who report bullying others (15%). The pervasiveness of distress associated with victimization at the hands of peers was highlighted by a recent survey of 2,000 children aged 10 to 16. For every one child concerned about being sexually abused by adults, there were three children concerned about being beaten up by peers. (2001, 242)

Holt and Keyes estimate an even higher number. When one considers bully, victim, and bully/victim involvement in the bullying encounter, they contend nearly 30% of children are included in one of these categories (2004, 121). Research by Kochenderfer and Ladd (1996) asserts that such bullying is evident in the earliest grades of schooling. Interviewing a sample of some 200 kindergarteners (105 males and 95 females) some 20.5% indicated that they had been repeatedly victimized by others. In a large study of eighty-six Australian schools by Ken Rigby (1997a) nearly 38,000 students were surveyed (22,194 boys and 15,703 girls—average age: 13.8 years) 22% of the boys and 16% of the girls admitted to being bullied at least once a week—with another 27.3% and 26.2% (respectively) indicating they also had been bullied, but in a less frequent manner. Hoover, Oliver, and Hazler (1992) indicate even higher percent ages. When students were asked if they had *ever* been bullied in their school years, their research found that 81% of males and 72% of females had, indeed, experienced bullying in one form or another (cited in

Hanish et al. 2004, 141). Focusing on the subtleties of relational aggression, Rachel Simmons indicates that, at least among women, destructive relational dynamics are widespread and endemic. Yet, because of their hidden nature relational bullying encounters are often simply undetectable (2002). Recent research in Washington State indicates that even though anti-bullying laws are on the books and most schools/districts require anti-bullying training and policies, the level of bullying activity has remained steady (Kester and Mann 2008, i). Bullying continues to be pervasive in schools around the world, resisting strategies, programs, and policies aimed at its eradication.

Consequences

Olweus reminds us that "being a bully or a victim is something that can last for a long time, often for several years" (1993, 27). His research has found that "Approximately 60% of boys who were characterized as bullies in grades 6–9 had at least one [criminal] conviction by the age of 24. Even more dramatically, as much as 35–40% of the former bullies had three or more convictions by this age, while this was true of only 10% of the control [non-bullying] boys" (1993, 36). Atlas and Pepler contend that their research, examining the continuity between adolescent and adult bullying, "revealed that bullying at age 14 predicts bullying at age 32" (1998, 93). Rigby, citing a study of bullies between the ages of 13 and 16, asserts that "the degree to which Australian male students (n=338) engaged in bullying others correlated significantly with mental ill health scores" (2002, 115–116). This study indicated that male bullies exhibited increased somatic disorder, anxiety, poor coping skills, and depression.[3] Females—in the same age range from the same schools—also exhibited elevated scores in all indices except the "coping category". "Hence," Rigby contends, "there is reason to believe that adolescents who frequently engage in bullying others tend to be somewhat distressed" (2002, 116). Simmons reminds us that with aggression among girls, especially when it is bent on creating and maintaining the popularity of the bully, even the "in" girls live frantic lives, always defending their own status (2002). While more research is needed regarding the effects of bullying upon the bully, current research does indicate the negative impact such activities have upon the perpetrator. Bullying shapes the bully; tentatively establishing their own status, often predicting later illegal behavior, and is typically correlated with anxiety and depression.

Of course, the bulk of research regarding the effects of bullying has been directed toward the victim. Perry et al. contend:

> Chronic harassment by peers is associated with serious adjustment problems, including depression, anxiety, emotional disregulation, social withdrawal, low self-esteem, loneliness, suicidal tendencies, dislike and avoidance of school, poor academic performance, rejection by mainstream peers, and a lack of friends. (2001, 73)

Research has also found that victimization is a better predictor of school maladjustment, rather than maladjustment predicting bullying (Atlas and Pepler 1998). In support, Egan and Perry (1998) found that while low self-esteem was a significant predictor of victimization among the 189 eleven-year-olds in their study, being victimized by a bully also *caused* a loss of self-regard. The victim comes to believe that he or she is not very successful at interacting with others, lowering social confidence, thus increasing targetability by future bullies. Similar to bullies, victims also scored high on mental ill-health scores—indicating psychological distress in somatic disorders, anxiety, social dysfunction, and depression (Rigby 2002, 113). Research also indicates increased suicidal ideation (i.e., the frequency with which people think about taking their own lives) among those frequently victimized (Rigby and Slee 1999; Kaltialo-Heino et al. 1999). Vaernes, Myhre, Henrik, and Homnes contend that the continued stress of victimization may cause, in some students, a lowered resistance to infection as well as a host of other health maladies (1991). Boivin et al. outline the future ramifications of being victimized:

> In the last 20 years, an extensive research effort on childhood peer status has shown that children who are rejected by their peers are at risk for a variety of future adjustment problems, including both internalizing and externalizing difficulties, and dropping out of school. Behaviorally, results of a large-scale meta-analysis indicate that rejected children are more aggressive, more withdrawn, less sociable, and/or less cognitively skilled than their more accepted peers. (2001, 268)

Swearer, Grills, Hay and Cary point toward the depression and hopelessness that surface in the face of a lack of agency among victims: "they 'give up' because they believe that their behavior cannot influence their environment" (2004, 66). Not only do victims often give up, but they also often begin to believe that they are to blame. Victimization becomes internalized, thus diminishing self-regard and any real sense of agency (Rigby 2002, 124). Brown contends that female victims, and I would argue *all* victims, learn to live fraudulent lives in order to find acceptance:

> They [young women] are telling us that what they are encouraged to call love and friendship is contingent on the disappearance of core parts of themselves; that acceptance and inclusion by others is connected to self-effacement and fraudulence. (2003, 77)

Finally, in the wake of the school shootings of late, Espelage and Swearer claim that "71% [of the shooters] had been targets of a bully" (2003, 367). In an extended quote from a high school student's perspective, we gain a sense of the hopelessness and anger that can reside within the victim's experience:

Like most students [in high school], I lived in fear of the small slights and public humiliation used to enforce the rigid high school caste system ... Students lived in fear of physical violence. There was a boy named Marty at my school ... who was beaten up daily for years. Jocks would rip his clothes, knowing that his parents could not afford to buy him a new uniform, and he would piss his pants rather than risk being caught alone in the bathroom. He couldn't walk the halls without being called a fag, and a freshman would beat him up to impress older kids ... another kid I know was thrown through a plate-glass window by a jock when he was a sophomore. When his mother complained to the principal, she was told that if her son insisted on dressing the way he did ... he'd have to get used to being thrown through plate-glass windows. A jock jumped another friend of mine, beating the [***] out of him and breaking his nose. My friend never threw a punch, but he was suspended for fighting along with the jock ... While I didn't suffer the extreme abuse some of my friends did, I was [***]ed with enough to spend four years fantasizing about blowing up my high school and everyone in it ... How many kids are ostracized, humiliated, and assaulted in American high schools? ... so long as some kids go out of their way to make high school hell for others there are going to be kids who crack, and not all of the kids who crack are going to go quietly. (Phillips 2000, 161)

The effects of bullying on the victim are devastating, bringing loneliness and depression, decreasing interest in school, increasing suicidal ideation and fueling violence toward the perpetrators.

INDIVIDUAL CHARACTERISTICS OF BULLYING

The Bully

Of course trying to define the characteristics of a typical bully proves problematic from the start. What kind of bully should one try to define? Should we consider a student who bullies others physically? Research by Baron-Cohen et al. (1999) indicates that physical bullies have a more difficult time reading facial expressions than non-bullies. In other words, physical bullies seem to have some deficiency in reading social cues, especially when they are conveyed through the body language of others. But, this same research indicates that those who bully in other ways (e.g., verbal, socially) were average (i.e., scored similarly to non-bullies) in regards to picking up on such social cues. Such delineations of the characteristics of the "normal" bully, then, must be approached with caution and flexibility. With this caveat I now outline the literature regarding the general "make-up" of a typical bully, acknowledging that individual bullies may not fit the "norm" perfectly.

First, I consider bully self-image or self-regard. As indicated earlier bullies do, indeed, tend to score lower on mental health tests (Rigby 2002), but this may or may not be connected to self-regard. Many would argue in one of two directions regarding bully self-image. Ken Rigby contends that, "School children who bully are at least as likely as others to say, "I feel I don't have much to feel proud of"; and "at times I think I'm no good at all." They are no more likely than others to say "I am able to do things as well as most people"; and "on the whole I am satisfied with myself.' (Rigby 1997b). They are, alas for the theory, indistinguishable from non-bullies" (Rigby 2002, 134).

In contrast, research by O'Moore and Kirkham (2001) found that both bullies and victims maintained lower self-esteem when compared with others who were not involved in bullying. Tim Field argues both at once. Field characterizes bullies as insecure people with low self-esteem, but also students who see themselves as "wonderful, kind, caring and compassionate" (as noted by Rigby 2002, 134). These contradictory assessments confound any definitive understanding of the bully and self-regard.

Hence, research seems to indicate that while some bullies may report low self-esteem, in general low self-regard is not always a defining characteristic of the bully. While bully self-esteem is a cloudy issue, the literature does indicate, as discussed earlier, a higher rate of emotional distress. Bullies seem to be more depressed than non-bullies and, like victims, show signs of higher suicide ideation (Rigby 2002). Simply put, bullies seem to be less happy than non-bullies. Of course, a pertinent question here involves whether those mental markers are caused by their bullying or exist prior to bullying behavior. More research is necessary here.

Empathy, or a lack thereof, also remains a focal point regarding the bully. Citing current research, Kaukianinen et al. argue that "empathy has been found to inhibit or, at least, mitigate [bullying] aggression" (1999, 83). They define empathy in two ways: "(1) the awareness of another person's thoughts, feelings, and intentions and (2) the ability or tendency to be vicariously aroused by the affective state of another person" (1999, 83). Feshbach, mirroring this sentiment, defines empathy as "an emotional response that emanates from the emotional state of another individual, and although empathy is defined as a shared emotional response, it is contingent on cognitive as well as emotional factors" (1997, 35). In a study of 12–14 year-olds, Farley (1999) found that bullies scored lower on "perspective taking" than non-bullies.[4] Succinctly, bullies were less able than other students to understand life from the perspective of another or, when upset, to put themselves in the shoes of another. Bullies also scored lower on empathic concern, indicating that they were less emotionally affected or had less concerned feelings for others. Empathy in the literature seems also to be associated with prosocial behavior—though some studies do not sustain this link (Eisenberg and Miller 1987). Yet, Espelage, Mebane, and Adams argue that generally "the ability to experience the affect of others is associated with altruism or helping behaviors in even very young children and has been shown to increase in children following empathy training" (2004, 39). "Many bullying prevention programs," assert Espelage and Swearer,

> include empathy training based on the extensive literature documenting the role of empathy in suppressing aggression (Miller and Eisenberg, 1988). Research suggests that self-declared bullies sometimes report feeling sorry after bullying their peers (Borg, 1998). (2003, 373)

But research by Coke, Batson, and McDavis (1978) found that empathy was only linked to "helping behavior" when perspective taking was connected with empathetic emotion. Perspective taking in isolation did not increase helping behavior. Interestingly, we again see differentiations regarding the impact of empathy when focused upon different kinds of bullying. Empathy seems to do little to inhibit physical aggression. But it buffers against relational aggression (Espelage, Mebane, and Adams 2004). Research by Endresen and Olweus (2001) indicates a link—though weak—between empathy and bullying for both girls and boys—boys with a slightly lower correlation—but indicated a strong correlation between attitudes toward bullying and mediated bullying activity. Espelage and Swearer note that in their research Endresen and Olweus found

> ... that a positive attitude toward bullying mediated the association between empathic concern and the frequency of bullying others. In other words, respondents with high levels of empathic concern tended to view bullying as negative and therefore bullied others less. This mediation was found for both boys and girls. This study highlights the importance of considering attitudes toward bullying in understanding how empathy relates to this subset of aggression. (2003, 373)

In general, the literature describes the bully as one with lowered—though certainly not missing—levels of empathy. The building of, or training toward, empathy in the bully continues to be a popular approach in many anti-bullying programs and strategies.

As indicated earlier power dynamics are foundational in the bullying encounter. How does this reflect upon bully characteristics? Succinctly, bullies are typically stronger than their victims, either physically or in some other way (Olweus 1993; Perry et al. 2001). In fact Olweus argues that physical strength "is quite significant in determining the popularity of a boy. And [that] popularity is likely to decrease a boy's risk of being bullied" (1993, 37). Lynn Mikel Brown, critiquing male-dominated views of bullying, interjects issues of gender and race, arguing that other types of power or strength (in addition to physical strength) play into the bullying relationship. Brown contends that "belonging gives girls the power to exclude all those 'others' who don't fit in—and, ... belonging has much to do with race, class, sexual identity, physical ability and appearance" (2003, 185). In other words, the imbalance of power may exist on a number of levels (e.g., physically, relationally, sexually, economically, etc.).

Bullies may also have what Olweus calls an "aggressive reaction pattern" (1993, 35). By this, Olweus means that many bullies are not only aggressive toward their victims, but toward others as well (e.g. adults, other students). Salmivalli and Nieminen delineate this aggression into categories of proactive and reactive aggression (mentioned earlier), surfacing such tendencies in both bullies and victims, and those who have been termed bully-victims. In their study of types of bullying aggression they found that bullies in *aggregate* "scored high on both types of aggression [proactive and reactive]," but that *individual* bullies may not always exhibit both (2002, 42). In fact, bullies were represented in three ways: reactively aggressive, proactively aggressive, and reactively-proactively aggressive. They contend that,

> Identifying these subgroups of bullies has practical implications: determining whether a reactive or proactive tendency is predominant in a bully might be central in choosing the most appropriate intervention strategy. (2002, 42)

Salmivalli and Nieminen's research, though, finds that most bullies are proactively aggressive. They contend that "emotional arousal or feelings of anger are not necessarily involved in bullying behavior. No external provocation is necessarily present either. Rather, bullying can be seen as an institutionalized habit, or 'cool' aggression" (2002, 32). The most aggressive bullying category seems to be the bully-victim. This person is one who serves a dual role: s/he is both a bully (aggressing instrumentally toward others) and also a victim (the target of other bullies). Here, Salmivalli and Nieminen argue that "bully-victims constituted the most aggressive group of all," and that they were "highly aggressive both reactively *and* proactively" (2002, 42).

In addition to these characteristics bullies may maintain good grades or struggle academically (Olweus 1993). Bullies seem to focus on establishing dominance (Pellegrini and Long 2004).[5] Bullies may be well liked, even popular (Simmons 2002), or may remain on the margins of status (Furlong et al. 2003). The bully may lack social intelligence or have good social skills (Kaukiainen et al. 1999).[6] Some studies do indicate that bullies are more likely than non-bullies to dislike working with others on collaborative projects and are more uncooperative (Rigby, Cox, and Black 1997). Bullies may also feel sorry for their victims (Espelage and Swearer 2003) or they may not (O'Connell et al. 1999).

Finally, Olweus' research finds that family characteristics, as well as child temperament, play a distinct role in the formation of the bully. He argues that:

> First, the basic emotional attitude of the parents, mainly that of the primary caretaker (usually the mother), toward the boy is very important, maybe in particular the emotional attitude during his earlier years. A negative basic attitude, characterized by lack of warmth and involvement, clearly increases the risk that the boy will later become aggressive and hostile toward others. A second important factor is the extent to which the primary caretaker has been permissive and allowed aggressive behavior on the part of the child. . . . We can summarize these results by stating that too little love and care and too much "freedom" in childhood are conditions that strongly contribute to the development of an aggressive reaction pattern. . . . A third factor that has been found to raise the child's level of aggression is the parent's use of "power-assertive" childrearing methods such as physical punishment and violent emotional outbursts. (1993, 39–40)

Research indicates a link "between general aggressive behavior in youth and lack of family cohesion" (Espelage and Swearer 2003, 376; Hanish et al. 2004). Earlier I mentioned that the bully seems to be less interested in cooperative group efforts—hence, underscoring, perhaps, a relationally "disconnected" aspect of the bully's experience. Renae Duncan delineates four specific styles of parenting that may play into the creation of the bully: authoritarian (demanding and unresponsive); authoritative (demanding and responsive); indulgent (responsive, yet undemanding); and indifferent (undemanding and unresponsive) (2004). Duncan's research suggests that:

> Children whose parents use authoritarian styles tend to be either aggressive toward their peers [bullies] or dominated by peers [victims]. Similarly, children whose parents are permissive tend to be aggressive [bullies], especially when their parents fail to place limits on aggressive behaviors, and the children of uninvolved parents are likely to display aggressive [bullies] and delinquent behavior. In contrast, children whose parents use more authoritative styles tend to be independent and to have strong social skills. (2004, 232)

Duncan offers insight into the roles of "connection" and "guidance" in the formation of both bullies and victims. Her findings indicate that parental responsiveness coupled with behavioral expectations foster independence and good social skills in children. Where there is a lack of interest (or connection) within the family, aggressing or being aggressed against seems to be more likely. Bowers et al. support this view adding that "it is as if these bullies are developing a general model of relationships as lacking warmth, and concerned with power" (1994, 228).

In summary, bullies seem to come in a variety of shapes and aptitudes, can be popular or not, and often come from families that are domineering, lack connection, and/or are permissive. Generally bullies seem to exhibit mental health troubles (e.g., depression, anxiety), may have lower self-regard, lack certain elements of empathetic response (e.g., perspective taking, concerned feelings toward others), and often have propensities toward proactive aggression. Bullies typically use their more powerful position to intentionally dominate a more vulnerable victim. Bullies also seem to often have a difficult time connecting with others or tend to resist cooperative endeavors.

Jake was a popular student at Southside. He was expected to excel, as his older brothers had done, in everything he put his hand to. Yet, his efforts, though admired by others, always seemed to pale—in his own eyes and in the eyes of his parents—when compared to his siblings. Jake's parents could be demanding. Jake had a lot to live up to. Sammy was aggressive, quick to get angry, and insecure. He struggled academically and lived with demanding and exacting parents. He, too, lived in the shadow of a sibling. Jeff was an only child; sensitive and indulged. He struggled academically and athletically. He masked the pain of being a step behind, felt deeply by him, with male bravado and a reckless abandon. Many of the findings forwarded by the current research are, indeed, evident in this trio that fashioned a game of bump intended to humiliate a "weaker" classmate.

THE VICTIM

Regarding victims of bullying Olweus asserts that:

> The typical victims are more anxious and insecure than students in general. Further, they are often cautious, sensitive, and quiet. When attacked by other students, they commonly react by crying (at least in the lower grades) and withdrawal. Also victims suffer from low self-esteem, and they have a negative view of themselves and their situation. They often look upon themselves as failures and feel stupid, ashamed, and unattractive. (1993, 32)

Egan and Perry hypothesize that four characteristics within the victim's low self-concept were salient regarding the victim's propensity toward victimization. First, lower self-worth may cause the victim to "hesitate to assert their needs or to defend themselves during conflicts" (thus, becoming passive toward their aggressors). Lower self-worth also may bring to the victim a propensity to "expect and accept . . . negative feedback more than do people with high self-regard" (thus, carrying a willingness to be victimized). Lower self-regard is associated with "depression, cautiousness, and poor self-regulation" as well (thus, signaling vulnerability to peers). Finally "the fact that children with insecure, preoccupied attachments to their caregivers tend to be victimized by peers is consistent with the thesis that low self-esteem helps mediate victimization because poor self-concept is a hallmark characteristic of children with such anxious attachments" (1998, 299–300). Egan and Perry summarize these understandings:

> At present, our best guess is that low self-perceived peer social competence predicts victimization partly because it is associated with specific behavioral incompetencies exhibited during peer conflicts (e.g. submission, emotional disregulation), partly because it leads children to project a self-deprecating identity that invites abuse, and partly because it is associated with a low social position in the peer group that signals to aggressors likely impunity for attacking. (1998, 306)

Although early research argued that victims were not victimized because of extrinsic characteristics (e.g., wearing glasses, stuttering) (Olweus 1993), more recent research refutes this finding indicating that victims are often targeted because of specific physical or relational traits, e.g., weight (Janssen et al. 2004); physical size or strength (Egan and Perry 1998); academic skills (Atlas and Pepler 1998). The victim is targeted because s/he is "targetable." In other words, if physical or emotional attributes stand out (e.g., Matthew's propensity to cry) these become potential doorways to victimization. But not all who stand out are bullied; in fact, some who stand out become trendsetters, influencing new styles, attitudes, or interests. Here, three additional victim characteristics are important.

The first characteristic, mentioned earlier, involves passivity, as well as its twin *reactive* aggression. Passivity, or a lack of assertiveness, makes the victim an easier target for the bully (i.e., one who will not fight back). In support of this Beate Schuster finds that:

> Children who are victims of peer harassment were shown to be highly cooperative, to an extent that may indicate submissiveness. By contrast, children who are rejected but not victimized display the other extreme. They behave very competitively [one might say aggressively]. Children who suffer from neither rejection nor victimization are in between these two extremes. (2001, 306)

In contrast Schwartz et al., expanding on this view, assert that, "although the majority of these children [victims] tend to be characterized by submissive and passive behavioral tendencies, a subgroup of victims are prone toward aggressive or hostile behaviors" (2001, 147). Continuing, they contend that

> the research to date indicates that aggressive victims form a distinct group from bullies and passive victims, with a unique set of underlying mechanisms influencing their social development and adjustment. This impulsive, emotionally reactive, and dysregulated aggressive behavior differs from the goal-oriented and effective aggressive strategies

of bullies, as well as from the withdrawn and submissive behavior of passive victims. Perhaps as a result of their impaired self-regulation abilities, these children may be vulnerable to maladjustment in multiple domains of functioning. (2001, 164)[7]

Again, Schwartz et al. underline the particular hardship of aggressive victims, contending that "aggressive victims are among the most highly rejected children" (2001, 167). Clearly, though, the passive victim is the more common and is characterized by cautiousness, sensitivity, insecurity, diminished social skills, and a lack of friends.

A second salient characteristic to victimization involves the family. As either authoritarian or permissive parental-child relationships may foster the aggression of the bully, so family relational styles may also develop a propensity toward victimization. Remember, Duncan contends that "children whose parents use authoritarian styles tend to be either aggressive toward their peers or dominated by their peers" and that "children whose parents are permissive [also] tend to be aggressive" (2004, 232). Perry et al., concur, arguing that children with histories of insecure attachment are more at risk to "serve as target[s] of peer aggression" (2001, 83). Authoritarian parents may foster passivity within their children, the same passivity that characterizes a majority of victims. On the other hand, permissive parents—those who specifically fail to place limits on aggressive behavior—may allow for the uncontrolled reactive aggression attributed to the aggressive victim. Even the nature of sibling relations may play into victim propensity (Duncan 2004, 238).

Finally, research indicates that victims lack supportive friends that might come to their aid in fending off or deterring bullying advances. Egan and Perry argue that "most victimized children also lack the social competencies that make one a valued member of the peer group, such as friendliness, cooperativeness, prosocial skills, and a sense of humor" (1998, 299). In part, they infer that an inability to maintain friendships (i.e., becoming a valued member of a peer group), perhaps due to a lack of prosocial skills, invites victimization. Smith et al. quoting research by Hodges, Malone, and Perry (1997) argue that "there are three friendship/social network factors that moderate the risk of victimization: numbers of friends, quality of friends (such as their peer status), and general standing in the peer group (specifically, extent of peer rejection)" (2001, 338). Yet, Simmons argues that in some forms of bullying the victim is within the friendship circle of the bully (2002). It may not simply be a friend, or the number of friends one has that creates a buffer against victimization, but as Boulton et al. (1999) suggest, the identity, quality, and status of those friendships may prove to be the decisive factor.

In summary, the victim may be characterized as passive, or perhaps ineffectually aggressive, as insecure—he or she may have low self-esteem, may have some targetable attribute (e.g., overweight), may come from an authoritarian or permissive family, may have strained familial relationships, and may be friendless or at least not have friends of the right sort. Of course Matthew did not have all of these characteristics, but several may have combined inviting his victimization (sensitivity, passivity, a propensity to cry, etc.) As we have sought to consider the individual characteristics involved in bullying, O'Connell et al. remind us that "researchers have often overlooked the fact that, like other forms of aggression, bullying occurs within a social context. . . . The social behaviors of individuals and dyads unfold in the context of larger social settings which influence the interactions among individuals" (1999, 438).

GROUP CHARACTERISTICS OF BULLYING

> The themes of individual submission to group pressure, the conflict of conscience and authority, and the constructive role that groups have on the individual seem to be central to an individual's experience with the social world. (Milgram 1992, 198)

On several levels bullying can be characterized as a group process. Brown et al. (1994), referring to the extensive literature on peer relations and social group processes, outline the importance of "crowds" and their effect on group and individual identity and interaction. "Crowds refer to collections of adolescents identified by the interests, attitudes, abilities, and/or personal characteristics they have in common" (Brown et al. 1994, 123). "Crowds," they continue, "have two major functions: They structure [an] individual's development of identity or self-concept, and they structure social interactions" (1994, 124). Hence, crowds structure who adolescents interact with, who they are separated from,[8] (and the nature of those interactions), as well as how they come to see themselves. Once group membership is established, a significant importance is placed by members on similarities and differences among their group and others. "The exaggerated images," Brown et al. continue,

> of the "in-group's" strengths and the "out-group's" shortcomings are worked out and reinforced through in-group interactions; that is, they are consensually validated. Their expression reaffirms group membership and builds the solidarity of the group as a whole. (1994, 129)

Hence, it is through the "othering" of other groups that in-group membership is solidified. The status of one's own crowd is established through denigrating outside crowds and, thus, individual outsiders. Thus, crowds structure student relationships. Brown et al. contend, these crowd dynamics "channel adolescents into relationships with certain peers and away from interactions with others" (1994, 133). Additionally crowds not only involve the demarcations of who is 'in' and who is 'out' and who relates to whom, but also formulate hierarchies of status and desirability. Brown et al. contend,

> To be sure, desirability is related to status: the higher a crowd is on the status hierarchy, the more desirable it is. . . . Thus students' efforts to avoid associating with its [a crowd of lower status] members could be interpreted as more evidence that desirability simply reflects peer status. (1994, 146–147)[9]

In sum, four constructs become critical to understanding inter-crowd peer relations:

First, crowds are an inherently relational construct.

Second, adolescents use crowds to construct a symbolic road map of prototypic peer relations.

Third, a teenager's crowd affiliation and understanding of the crowd system affect the choice of peer associates and the features of peer relationships.

[Fourth], the crowd system is a dynamic phenomenon that is sensitive to contextual features of a social milieu. (Brown et al. 1994, 161–163)

Crowds, then, create a hierarchy of groups; one crowd is of higher status when compared to another, thus making inter-crowd movement difficult if not, at times, nearly impossible.

Long and Pellegrini (2003) help us to consider not only inter-group hierarchical status, but in-group hierarchies within peer social networks. Drawing on the literature on social dominance, they contend:

> From a group-level perspective, social dominance is a relational variable that orders individuals in a hierarchy according to their access to resources. . . . Dominance, or group leadership, is established when groups are newly forming (e.g., when groups form in new schools) or when extant groups are in a state of flux (new members are added or some members grow in size). Individuals compete with each other using both aggressive and affiliative strategies to gain status. (2003, 402)

Dominance, accordingly, is not an end in and of itself. It is focused on securing certain resources. In young children this may be a toy. In older adolescents it may be popularity or access to the opposite sex. Dominance may be a move to secure status itself.

> Bullying is viewed as an agonistic strategy used to obtain and maintain dominance (Bjorklund and Pellegrini, 2002). There is evidence that bullying is a successful strategy for attaining and maintaining dominance as individuals who get the better of their peers are often leaders of peer cliques and are found to be more attractive to the opposite sex (Pellegrini and Bartini, 2001; Pellegrini and Long, 2003; Prinstein and Cohen, 2001; Sutton, Smith, and Swettenham, 1999). Further, dominant individuals use affiliative strategies, such as reconciliation and alliance building, after status has been exhibited (Pellegrini and Bartini, 2001; Strayer, 1980). (Long and Pellegrini 2003, 402)

Thus, a bully may bully his friends or outsiders to prove he is a leader (or to establish his leadership), but then seek to reconcile with the victim to retain status and leadership in the eyes of his peers and in the eyes of the victim.

Hawker and Boulton, referring to the social rank literature, draw on Chance's (1988) description of group behavior. Some groups, they argue, operate on an *agonic* mode or style of establishing intra-group peer hierarchies. "In the agonic mode," they explain, "social power is determined by an individual's *resource-holding potential*. In other words, the dominant animal is the one who is toughest and wins the most fights" (2001, 382). Hence, students who are physically dominant have "high resource-holding potential," affording them privilege and status. Some groups operate on more of a *hedonic* mode. "In the hedonic mode social power is determined by social attention-holding power. For example, Gilbert (1992) has argued that humans tend to achieve status by showing that they are talented, knowledgeable, attractive, and so on, and that the highest-ranking humans . . . tend to receive the most attention from others" (in Hawker and Boulton 2001, 382). Simply put, both agonic and hedonic modes are operationalized within peer circles in order to establish rank, underscoring the importance of the group in establishing individual status. Yet, do we see evidence more commonly of "mobbing" (Olweus 1993)—groups bullying an individual (e.g., the bump crowd targeting Matthew) or of individual bullying—dyadically bullying another (e.g., Sammy and Matthew in a one-on-one bullying encounter)?

In a 1997 study by Ken Rigby aimed at understanding the prevalence of group versus individual bullying, it was reported that 44% of those interviewed were not bullied in anyway during the school year. 22%—the next most common experience—indicated that they had been bullied (though not often) "by individuals, but never by a group. Some 16% reported that they had been bullied sometimes by both" (1997b, 59). This research indicates that, unlike the Southside incident, it is more common for an individual bully to bully an individual student.[10] Yet, while there is evidence that bullying individuals may be more common than bullying groups, research indicates that bullying seldom takes place apart from the view of peers. Underscoring the group dynamics inherent in the phenomenon of bullying Sutton and Smith, while affirming that bullying is a dyadic process (i.e., between the bully and the victim), also contend that "bullying is collective in its nature, based on social relationships in the group" (1999, 97). "Pepler and Craig (1995)", they continue, "reported that peers were present in 85% of bullying episodes" (1999, 97–98). Referring to this group presence during the bullying episode, they go on to contend that,

> One fifth of pupils report that they might join in if they saw someone being bullied, and it seems that this reported attitude is often translated into actual support for the Bully. Do they reinforce the bullying, either by actively encouraging the Bully (perhaps by shouting or cheering when someone is being picked on [as was the case with Matthew and the bump game]) or by implying passive acceptance of the behavior (perhaps by usually being present when someone is picked on, without doing anything to stop it)? Twenty-three % of children report being amused by bullying scenarios. Peer onlookers joining in or reinforcing the bullying in these ways may be important to the Bully in that they inflate the Bully's self-esteem. Indeed, it is perhaps unsurprising that the most common reported motivations to Bully are "to feel powerful" or "to look cool". . . . Similarly peer onlookers may also spread the word that the Bully is powerful, thereby raising the Bully's social status (Sutton and Smith 1999, 98).

Interestingly, perhaps because many victims are cast as outcasts by the school social community, most schoolmates see the victim as deserving the bullying that he or she is experiencing (Juvonen and Graham 2001, 61). Owens et al. suggest that in their research there "appeared to be two main categories of responses that concerned the perceived characteristics of victims: first, that it was the victim's own fault, and second, that the victims were vulnerable or easy targets" (2001, 223). Sutton and Smith concur with the work of Salmivalli et al. (1996) regarding the social roles involved in the bullying phenomenon and their importance regarding both status and intervention. This research surfaces the following roles within the bullying dynamic:

> Bully (14%): starts bullying; gets others to join in bullying; always thinks of new ways of picking on the victim; leads a gang.

> Reinforcer (6%): is usually there; even if not doing anything; laughs at people getting bullied; encourages the bully by shouting; says things to the bully like "show him!"; gets others to watch.

> Assistant (7%): helps the bully, maybe by catching or holding the victim; joins in the bullying if someone else has started it.

> Defender (28%): tells some adult about the bullying; tries to make others stop the bullying; tries to cheer the victim up; gets others to help; sticks up for the victim.

Outsider (12%): isn't usually there, stays away; pretends not to notice what is happening; doesn't do anything or take sides; doesn't even know about the bullying.

Victim (18%): gets bullied

No Role (15%) (1999, appendix, percentages cited in Sutton and Smith and based on Salmivalli et al. 1996).

This research, then, underlines the fact that bullying is not only a dyadic phenomenon, involving the individual characteristics of and relations between bully and victim, but that bullying also involves a host of secondary roles within the larger peer structures of the school. O'Connell et al. elaborate:

> Bullies had a direct effect on peers: peers spent more than one-fifth of their time (21%) in actively joining with the bully to abuse the victim. This relatively high frequency of actively reinforcing the bully can be understood if we acknowledge that the playground context is ripe for modeling: the bully is powerful, teachers and peers seldom intervene, and peers can share in the bully's status and power by becoming accomplices. (1999, 447)

Bullying is situated within insider/outsider dichotomies, crowd, and interpersonal hierarchies, and moves to secure group status among crowds and individual status within groups. Salmivalli is pertinent here:

> The concept of social role seems to capture something essential here. Social roles have been defined as clusters of socially defined expectancies that individuals in a given situation are expected to fulfill. Seen from this point of view, participant roles, as roles in general—arise in social interactions and are determined by both individual behavioural dispositions and the expectations of others. (1999, 454)

In some ways peer relations become policing agencies within school culture. Peers, in association with the bully (or bullies) create an insider/outsider dynamic. In fact, one of the most damaging aspects of bullying in the victim's life comes from his or her isolation. Being cast outside by a peer group seems to be part and parcel of the bullying experience. The bullying encounter is situated in social interactions involving a wide variety of people within the school, many of whom use the encounter to gain status. Peer perception, both toward the bully and the victim, seems to play a significant role in the bullying dynamic. Again, research shows that friends are perhaps the greatest deterrent to becoming a victim. Perhaps this is because the bully is less likely to attack a victim whose friends will stand up for him or her (the victim becomes a less easy target), or because the status of the victim is raised by friendship with "acceptable" people, or perhaps because the connection within a friendship circle allows for ongoing development of relational skills within the victim, thus insulating him or her from social awkwardness. "Friends, by definition, share a warm and helping reciprocal relationship" (Boulton et al. 1999, 466), thus constructing a wall of protection against victimization by the peer community.

It is important to add here that not all victims follow the same relational path. The victim may begin as part of a crowd and then be cast from that crowd or smaller peer circle[11]. The victim may be an outlier (i.e., an outcast from the outset), having never been included in the bully's crowd, becoming a target for any number of reasons (physical appearance, reactive aggression, etc.). The victim may also be a part of a certain crowd or smaller peer circle and, in the course of bullying, remain within that peer crowd or circle. The bullying here, rather than casting the victim out of the group, simply is employed to establish hierarchy within that crowd or smaller peer circle. One might argue that the policing of the victim by the peer culture is bent on more than the annoying habits of the victim or a propensity to cry. In the insider/outsider dynamic, power and status are at play and the peer community becomes, at the beckon call of the bully, the enforcer of the borders of privilege (i.e., who is deemed acceptable and who is not).

GENDER AND BULLYING

One of the borders that bullying activity interacts with is that of gender. Dan Olweus asserts that "boys were more often victims and in particular perpetrators of direct bullying" (1993, 19). Olweus, regarding gender and bullying, continues:

> It should be recalled in this connection that girls were exposed to indirect bullying to about the same extent as boys. In addition, it is possible that some forms of bullying used by girls are so subtle that we have not been able to detect them with our questionnaire (though it is an unlikely possibility). (1993, 19–20)

Until recently bullying has predominately been seen as a male activity, situated in physical or verbal violence. According to Deborah Phillips (2000) boys have been "constructed" in our culture as aggressive and violent. According to Simmons (2002), similarly, girls have been "deemed" passive and nice by the norming voices of society. Boys aggress and bully, girls simply watch. Girls are "catty" and "bitchy"; boys are "physical" and "violent". Espelage and Swearer pick up on this gendered understanding:

> Are boys more aggressive than girls? Although a tremendous amount of research over the last several decades supports an answer of

"yes," ... more recent research would also support an answer of "it depends." ... That is, it depends on important contextual factors that might vary across investigations such as the definition of aggression, the method of assessment employed, and the age of the child/adolescent. (2004, 15)

They go on, in fact, to conclude that female aggression while perhaps differently nuanced, is very much a part of daily interaction:

When researchers challenged the traditional view that boys are more overtly aggressive than girls by broadening the definition of aggression to include less overt forms of aggression [which may not show up on Olweus' questionnaire], the result was an explosion of important research exploring the gender differences that traditionally emerged in the study of aggression. ... Findings from these studies support the idea that relational aggression is a form of aggression that is distinct from overt aggression and plays a unique role in youth psychological and social adjustment. (Espelage and Swearer 2004, 31)

Research indicates varying findings regarding gender and relational aggression. Using peer nominations to group students into four categories (relationally aggressive, overtly aggressive, both overtly and relationally aggressive, and nonaggressive) one study indicates that the nonaggressive group showed no sex difference (73.0% of boys; 78.3% of girls), that the males tended to be more overtly aggressive and that girls were more relationally aggressive (referenced in Espelage and Swearer 2003, 371). Other studies, though confirming that boys were more overtly aggressive and girls were more prosocial, nonetheless found that there were "no sex differences in relational aggression" (referenced in Espelage and Swearer 2003, 372).

In terms of victimization, research indicates that most bullying occurs within gender groups. Cross-gender bullying, when it does occur, typically involves boys bullying girls (Rigby 2002). Girls seem to be the victims of indirect bullying more than boys, especially from other girls. Boys, though, are also targets of indirect bullying, typically more often at the hands of girls than other boys. Physical bullying, although perpetrated at times by girls, is more prevalent among male bullies and is more often directed toward male victims (Rigby 2002). Interestingly, we do find evidence that in female single-sex schools the occurrence of bullying activity is diminished (Rigby 2002). Of course, as mentioned above, the prevalence of male and female bullying is hard to measure because of differences in tactics and means according to gender.

Phillips and Simmons contend that the differences we do see in the way that bullying transpires (direct versus indirect) has less to do with biology than with the ways culture constructs male and female identities. Phillips, speaking of scripted male construction asserts:

> Violent practices like sexual harassment of other boys and girls are a resource for masculine subjectivity production. They are productive in the sense that they create what they signify, the superior, tough, strong, and being in control norm of hegemonic white heterosexual masculinity. (2000, 162)

Acts of violence, according to Phillips, become equated or associated with "maleness". Boys simply employ the cultural scripts available to them. Indeed, statistics reveal that violence around the world has "overwhelmingly involved men and [is perpetrated] against men. Physical violence is a tacit avenue that can be taken up by males in order to demonstrate that one is a 'man'" (Phillips 2000, 6). Phillips contends that this construction of the male norm, based on a white, heterosexual viewpoint, includes characteristics of "superiority, being in control, toughness, strength, autonomy, competition, mastery, [and need for] getting respect" (2000, 6).

One might argue, then, that the binary opposite, "femaleness," would be characterized by inferiority, lack of control, fragility, dependence, non-competitiveness, weakness, and physical non-aggression. Simmons, in depicting the world of girls, confirms this alternate construction of girls. She argues that our culture, in contrast to masculine scripts, casts girls as nice and compliant. "It is precisely girls' reputation for civility which provides the perfect cover for covert aggressors, giving them unrestricted movement beneath the radar" (Simmons 2002, 226). In a culture that discourages competition and meanness among girls (casting mean girls as bitchy, promiscuous girls as sluts, and competitive girls as bossy), the aggressional patterns of girls more often operate in hidden ways. Simmons continues, "our culture refuses girls access to open conflict, and it forces their aggression into nonphysical, indirect, and covert forms (2002, 3). Lyn Mikel Brown concurs with Simmons' understanding:

> The prohibition against saying mean things [for girls], which seems to include any strong feelings or direct expression of opinion, means that most things are taken underground or out of relationship—or said behind others' backs. (2003, 128)

The proposed solutions to these gendered avenues into bullying focus on opening up new scripts. For example, Phillips calls for not only understanding the cultural motivations behind male violence, but for creating new cultural stories that will allow males different avenues of expression of their aggression (perhaps similar to current female scripts). Simmons, while also offering new insights into the cultural motivations behind female aggression, similarly calls for the creation of new female stories, allowing for the expression of anger and conflict (similar to a current male script). Important here is the understanding that, while gender certainly offers varying and tightly controlled avenues for expression, the studies of Phillips and Simmons ultimately confirm that bullying is evident in both males and females. We cannot simply say bullying is a *guy thing*, or that social aggression is a *girl thing*. In fact, since both males and females are actively involved in bullying encounters, granted employing different methodologies and strategies, we realize that bullying is a larger phenomenon which transgresses narrow gendered boundaries. New scripts for girls (e.g. an ability to express conflict) simply may change their bullying to become more direct. New scripts for boys (e.g. an ability to express aggression relationally instead of physically) simply may change their bullying to become more indirect. The issue, here, is, "why?" What are the motivations of bullying that end up being employed—granted along gendered lines—but nonetheless employed on a regular basis?

MOTIVATIONS OF BULLYING

Why do bullies bully? For the sake of clarity I will organize motivations outlined in the literature under five categories. Of course, some nuance is lost in such a grouping—motivations quickly cross and encompass the lines we establish—but, such a framing allows us to consider broadly the fires that fuel bullying activity. I organize the research on bullying motivation under five subheadings: misunderstanding, skill deficiency, status dominance, individual delinquency and environmental norming.

First, school bullying is often depicted as resting in individual misunderstanding, prompting informational anti-bullying approaches. Such misunderstanding can be characterized along two lines. First, we imagine such misunderstanding situated in the notion that the bully is not aware of or does not understand the policy, rules, definitions, damages caused by, and consequences of bullying activities. While not typically listed as a "characteristic of the bully", this sense of bullying as "misunderstanding" is made concrete within current anti-bullying strategies. Here, a lack of understanding of some sort becomes integral to bullying activities. Additionally, recalling our earlier discussion of empathy, a second "misunderstanding" is characterized within the literature. Empathy, or an awareness of the "thoughts, feelings, and intentions of another", has been linked by some to "inhibit or, at least, mitigate [bullying] aggression" (Kaukianinen et al. 1999, 83). Linked to empathy is the corollary of perspective-taking (i.e., the ability to see life from the perspective of another, to understand the way another sees, feels, experiences something) (Farley 1999). This view includes the notion that the bully simply may not understand the pain that bullying causes in the life of the victim. Bullying, then, becomes motivated by a lack of understanding toward the victim (Espelage, Membane, and Adams 2004, 39–58). One might argue here that Jake (taking satisfaction in Matthew's tears) could not see or feel life from Matthew's perspective (i.e., that such tears were situated in humiliation and pain in Matthew's life). "If Jake could understand life from Matthew's perspective," this line of thinking argues, "he would cease his bullying activities." Hence, helping the bully "understand" the victim (via the development of empathy and perspective-taking) is an important component in many anti-bullying strategies.

Employing the rubric of bullying as a misunderstanding of school policy (definitions, rules, expectations, consequences) or the victim (empathy) we find a number of responses embedded within typical school anti-bullying approaches.[12] For example, many anti-bullying programs call for school-wide informational and articulation activities (e.g., articulating bullying definitions (Horne, et al. 2004; Whitaker, et al. 2004; Hoover and Oliver 1996), establishing and articulating rules and guidelines regarding bullying activities (Olweus 1993; Espelage and Swearer 2004; Hoover and Oliver 1996; Rigby 2002), and outlining punitive consequences for bullying activities (Olweus 1993; Espelage and Swearer 2004)). Here, anti-bullying strategies aim at supplementing student and staff understanding regarding the definitions and activities of bullying, as well as articulating rules, expectations, and consequences aimed toward regulating bullying.[13] Additionally, many programs also call for empathy training activities embedded in the assumption that in some way the bully does not understand the victim, his experiences, or the consequences of bullying activities in the victim's life (Hoover and Oliver 1996; *Pika's Common Concern Method* (in Hoover and Oliver 1996);[14] Rigby 2002)). Through role-playing and empathic training, many anti-bullying strategies work to help the bully better understand the victim and his or her experience.

In line with this "misunderstanding" view, the Southside administration developed an informational anti-bullying campaign, focused upon individuals involved in bullying as well as the general student population via the student handbook, individual and classroom discussions, all-school assemblies, and hallway banners. This informational approach was aimed at helping the school population understand what bullying entails, the harm it inflicts, and school behavioral guidelines regarding bullying activities. Jake and his friends were also required to undergo role-playing and empathy building exercises to increase perspective taking and their understanding of Matthew and the pain their activities were causing him.

Second, school bullying is often depicted as centered in individual skill deficiency, prompting training and supplementing anti-bullying approaches. Here, a lack of skill of some sort becomes integral to bullying activities for both victims and bullies. On the one hand, victims are depicted as potential targets because they lack friends, at least friends of a certain type (Espelage and Swearer 2004; Juvonen and Graham 2001, 80, 338) and, more foundationally, the skills to develop and maintain such friendships. Victims also are seen to have low self-esteem/self-regard (Olweus 1993, 33; Juvonen and Graham 2001, 78) or confidence (Doll, Song, and Siemers 2004, 172) requiring esteem/confidence building programs aimed toward supplementing such deficiencies. Some victims are victimized, it seems, because they are reactively aggressive—in other words, because they lack anger management skills (Olweus 1993, 33; Juvonen and Graham 2001, 306)—or, at times, because they lack social competence (Sheridan, Warnes, and Dowd 2004, 245–257) prompting aggression management or social competency training regimes. Research also finds that victims lack power (or at least are less powerful than their bullies (Olweus 1993, 32)), thus, lacking an ability to defend themselves (Doll, Song, and Siemers 2004, 163). Additionally, victims are often seen as passive (Olweus 1993, 32; Juvonen and Graham 2001, 77, 306), needing to undergo assertiveness training (Juvonen and Graham 2001, 347), and as anxiety ridden (Swearer et al. 2004, 69), lacking a sense of rest or peace with themselves and the world with in which they live, again, requiring a host of skill building programs.

On the other hand, the bully is depicted within the literature as lacking skill in important ways. A small %age may bully from an inability to control aggression. Whether from a lack of clear guidelines regarding aggression, or growing up in an abusive family, some bullies may struggle with outbursts of anger and aggression (Olweus 1993, 35), requiring anger or aggression management training. Some portray bullies as individuals lacking in social skills or social intelligence (Sheridan, Warnes, and Dowd 2004, 245–257), prompting social interaction and relational competency training. Here, students are taught skills to help them develop healthy peer relations, including basic social skills to enable them to help prevent and deal with bullying situations (Horne et al. 2004; Whitaker et al. 2004; Hoover and Oliver 1996). Additionally, the literature indicates that the bully may lack cohesive relationships in the home (Olweus 1993), requiring training regimes set in group projects and cooperative assignments, aimed at training toward better student connection within the school.

At Southside this skill-building approach was certainly employed. For Matthew, the training involved developing a more aggressive stance toward others, building stronger relational skills, ceasing to cry in public, etc. For the trio, the training involved aggression-management skills, empathetic skills, relational skills (including the nurturance of respect and care for others via discussion, role-playing, etc.), and better cooperative skills.

Third, school bullying is often depicted as centered in moves toward status dominance, prompting student training and status re-direction anti-bullying approaches (i.e., altering the ways students think about and secure power and status within the school setting). Pellegrini and Long argue that bullying "is a specific form of aggression and one that is used deliberately to secure resources" (2004, 109). What might these resources be? "Bullying seems to be used as a way in which boys [and I would argue girls as well] gain and maintain dominance status with peers" (2004, 110). Simmons, referencing the findings of Michael Thompson and colleagues, asserts that "every child wants three things out of life: connection, recognition, and power. The desire for connection," she continues, "propels children into friendship, while the need for recognition and power ignites competition and conflict" (2002, 9). Malecki and Demaray contend that "students' bullying behavior may actually increase (or at least not reduce) their peer support" (2004, 221). In other words the bully may be, in part, seeking to establish his or her own status within the peer community by casting the "other" as illegitimate. Anthony Pellegrini offers helpful insight on this assertion:

> Harassment is often public when perpetrators use it to display dominance over their peers. This sort of public display is especially evident during early adolescence, a time when social status is in a state of flux because of rapid physical changes and changes in social groups. (2001, 129)

Most bullying is witnessed by others. It often raises the bully's status in the eyes of many within his or her peer group. The bully often employs "associates," somewhat under his/her control, who gang up on the victim. Bullying, then, becomes a public power move, leaving the perpetrator more securely "inside" and the victim more clearly "outside". This is not to say that bullying does not take place privately, but even then one might argue that within the bully, the dominance over another, even if private, affords a sense of status exemplified in the unequal power balance. Both the bully and the victim, indeed, know who is in control and who is powerless. Remember that popularity is a significant insulator against victimization (Olweus 1993; Pellegrini and Long 2004), thus connecting status to both the victim and to the bully.

The literature more precisely envisions a number of nuances regarding status as an aim of bullying. Status often allows one to construct lines of inclusion—that is who is in and who is out (Simmons 2002; Brown 2003; Juvonen and Graham 2001, 225–226). Dominance, often associated with status, is depicted as a primary goal of bullying (Rigby 2002, 150; Pellegrini and Long 2004, 109–110). Such attempts at dominance are seen to become more sophisticated—perhaps more appropriate or simply more effective—as one grows older (Hawley 1999 in Rigby 2002, 150). High social status is often sought by the bully (Rodkin 2004, 94) offering certain benefits to the bully with peers (Pellegrini and Long 2004, 108–111)— especially as one negotiates group inclusion (Pellegrini and Long 2004, 112)—and offers the bully a certain amount of attention (Juvonen and Graham 2001, 224–225) and attractiveness (Espelage and Swearer 2003, 376). Even for the victim, higher status becomes a buffer *against* victimization (Juvonen and Graham 2001, 346), while low status becomes a pathway *to* victimization (Juvonen and Graham 2001, 270).

Hence, bullies (and victims), must be trained to develop better relational or status acquisition skills or aptitudes. For example, role-playing is used to develop social awareness and expertise (Olweus 1993; Espelage and

Swearer 2004); cooperative learning is featured within the classroom (similar and connected to the "skill building" articulated in skill-based anti-bullying programs alluded to above), including the facilitation of "positive common class activities" (Olweus 1993; Espelage and Swearer 2004); and students are trained to relate in respectful ways, thus seeking status by more appropriate means (Hoover and Oliver 1996; Rigby 2002). In our Southside example, the administration certainly sought to train Jake and his friends. Jake, Sammy and Jeff were trained in the proper use of power as well as directed toward more appropriate status-acquisition skills (e.g., gaining status by excelling on the sports field or academically instead of through the humiliation of another) and better cooperative skills (e.g., working in small groups, etc.).

Fourth, school bullying is often depicted as centered in individual rule-breaking, prompting punitive and rehabilitative anti-bullying approaches.[15] Here, the bully is depicted in some measure as a troubled, or even delinquent, individual; a "bad egg". This is not necessarily meant to disparage the bully, but to underline the desire of the bully intent on causing harm to another. Matthew's perpetrators seemed to take pleasure in the tears of their victim. The bully is thus in need of surveillance—because of their propensity to unprovoked violence (whether relational or physical), and rehabilitation—because of their pleasure in the pain of another. Bullies are individuals who must be watched, punished, and rehabilitated. They are problem students (Rigby 2002, 128–130) who, for any number of reasons seek social dominance. Some would argue they are "programmed" toward such activities through environment or nature itself (Rigby 2002, 150–151). Bullies can be depicted as anti-social and rule breakers (Olweus 1993, 35), students who must be disciplined, trained, and brought back into a position of healthy and appropriate social interaction.

This assumption is clearly articulated within the typical anti-bullying strategies. For example, increased supervision of bullies and their activities (as well as protectively toward victims) is called for (Olweus 1993, Espelage and Swearer 2004, Hoover and Oliver 1996, Alsaker and Valkanover 2001), clear rules and consequences of bullying activities are enacted (Olweus, Espelage and Swearer 2004; Horne et al. 2004; Whitaker et al. 2004; Hoover and Oliver 1996; Rigby 2002), and "stern talks" are directed toward the bully and his or her parents (Olweus 1993, Swearer et al. 2004. Again, the Southside administration sought to rehabilitate Jake and his accomplices employing many of these techniques. They were reprimanded, parents were called, sanctions were meted out, more serious sanctions were threatened (e.g., detentions and suspensions), and these students were watched (classroom and recess staff were alerted and asked to "keep an eye" on the trio).

Finally, school bullying is often depicted as centered in environmental or ecological norming, prompting whole school approaches (including peer culture, teacher attitudes, and relational climate). In other words, research suggests that bullies are formed environmentally, i.e., bullies are created in the home through parenting styles and family functioning—including issues of early parent-child bonding (Rigby 2002 156–168) and may be "re-formed" employing such environmental means. Research links bullying activities with a lack of parental closeness (Kasen et al. 2004, 200), inappropriate genetic tendencies, or parental example (O'Connor et al. 1980 in Rigby 2002, 152). Research indicates that peer ecologies—the ways peers interact, the ways status is enacted among groups, the attitudes of peers toward aggression—also deeply shape and motivate bullying activities (Duncan 2004, 232, 240; Juvonen and Graham 2001, 83–86; Hoover and Oliver 1996, 5). In fact, students may emulate or seek to exemplify bullying activities if the bully is afforded higher status through of such activities (Malecki and Demaray 2004, 216). Some also argue that how the larger culture views bullying or aggression (Rodkin 2004, 101), teacher attitudes (Holt and Keys 2004, 122–124; Espelage and Swearer 2003, 378), and school relational climate (Holt and Keyes 2004, 124–125) all may motivate bullying activity in some measure.

Hence, the culture of the school itself must be altered in order to bring transformation to the bully and school bullying activities. For example, the playground must be made more attractive, hoping to draw students into more healthy activities of play (Olweus 1993), school and home "milieus" are sought to be transformed (Olweus 1993; Espelage and Swearer 2004; Whitaker 2004; Hoover and Oliver 1996), organization of the school and classroom environment is promoted so as to leave "less room" for bullying (Horne et al. 2004), and peer culture is employed to put pressure on bullies to cease bullying activities as well as to create caring cultures within the school (Olweus 1993; Espelage and Swearer 2004; Alsaker and Valkanover 2001; Rigby 2002; Maines and Robinson 1992). Again, in our Southside story, school administrators sought to involve the families of the bullies not only to discipline their children, but to cultivate relational spaces in the home that might mitigate their student's bullying behavior. Peer counselors also were employed, working to help resolve student conflicts. Potential bullying sites were removed from the campus. The bump game was forbidden, and more cooperative activities at recess were encouraged. Finally, anti-bullying assemblies and motivational banners were employed, again seeking to create a culture within which bullying activity was discouraged.

SUMMARY

To recap, based upon the research literature outlined above, bullying is intentional activity that is repeated over time. It is targeted upon a weaker victim, and is thus situated in unequal power relations. It may employ verbal, physical, or social methodologies and is disruptive to learning and harmful to the victim and to the bully. Though it has dyadic elements, it is most often enmeshed in peer relations. Bullying is also shaped by cultural factors—such as gender. Bullying continues to be a pervasive element in the current school landscape. Bullying, finally, seems to be motivated by a number of issues—misunderstanding, skill deficiency, inappropriate status acquisition activities, delinquency, or ecological environing—resulting in a wide-range of individual, whole school and family strategies aimed against it.

According to the research Jake, Sammy and Jeff were bullies; Matthew was a victim. The trio possessed greater power than Matthew—physically, socially, or in some other way. This was certainly the case in their interactions. The trio intentionally targeted Matthew over the course of the entire year, encouraging others to join into the exclusion and ridicule. The bullying was devastating to Matthew, causing his grades to plummet, motivating him to miss school and raising thoughts of worthlessness and suicide in his thinking. Though the bullying at times looked dyadic (Jeff teasing/distaining Matthew when alone), it was primarily a social activity—drawing in the bump game, excluding Matthew from the group, etc. It was not only carried out socially—the group cheering at Matthew's exit from the bump game, it was also on display socially—most of the bullying was carried out in the context of other students knowing or watching. Each of the trio bullied out of a sense of insecurity (i.e., they had a lot to live up to) and the bullying offered a certain amount of concrete status over Matthew and with peers—the bump crowd loved Jake, Sammy and Jeff. They became heroes of sorts. A number of strategies were employed toward ending the bullying of Matthew. Jake, Sammy and Jeff were given information, they were trained in certain skill areas (as was Matthew), they were instructed to seek status in more acceptable ways, they were reprimanded and watched, and a school-wide informational and peer training plan was put in place. And yet, with a plethora of strategies aimed at stopping the bullying of Matthew, the bullying continued.[16] It only ended when Matthew left the school. Jake, Jeff and Sammy simply picked a new target the next year. Why did these strategies fail to stop the bullying? Are we missing something?

3 Current Anti-Bullying Work
A Fly in the Ointment

As outlined in Chapter 2, research indicates at least five general possibilities for bullying motivation. First, the bully may bully out a lack of understanding—whether a lack of clarity on school policy, bullying definitions, or rules; or a misunderstanding of the victim and his or her experience (i.e., empathy). Second, the bully may bully out of skill deficiency—whether social skill or an inability to regulate aggression of anger. Third, the bully may bully out of misdirected status acquisition attempts—seeking to establish popularity or gain privileges in inappropriate ways (i.e., through dominating or humiliating a classmate). Fourth, the bully may bully out of general delinquency—i.e., a malevolent will bent on causing pain and destruction in the lives of others. Finally, a bully may bully because he or she is a product of the environment within which bullying is allowed, modeled, or even encouraged (e.g., teachers that bully or turn a blind eye to bullying, family members that have modeled the behavior, etc.). This is not to suggest that current anti-bullying strategies are based upon the assumption that such motivations operate independently (i.e., anti-bullying strategies often respond to a number of these motivations in a more holistic manner), but that these form the main strains of bullying motivation as we've come to understand it.

ANTI-BULLYING STRATEGIES

Programs including "Bully Busters" (www.bullybusters.org), "Expect Respect" (www.safeplace.org), "Olweus" (www.olweus.org), Pika's "Common Concern Method" (www.education.unisa.edu.au/bullying/concern.html), "Steps to Respect" (www.cfchildren.org), to "Stop Bullying Now" (www.stopbullyingnow.com) are varied in their approaches and have been employed for a number of years across the country and around the world. While each program carries its own nuance, several main components form common themes across most programs. Typical anti-bullying efforts contain four major elements: Assessment—this involves gaining an 'on-the-ground' sense of how much bullying is actually happening within a school or setting, who is being targeted, and perhaps who is targeting and/

or participating in bullying activity. Such assessments may involve school-wide surveys or questionnaires, student interviews, student reporting, observational reports, or parent surveys.

Second, most programs include some type of direct response to those involved in active bullying. For example, bullies are reprimanded, educated, trained, offered incentives, and watched. Victims, likewise, are supported, trained, and watched. Peers that are involved in some ways are also brought into the fold of training, educating, and surveillance (including ways that peers can actively support victims).

Third, informational campaigns and whole-school training is enacted. The order of this listing isn't meant to imply that informational campaigns happen after direct response to bullies; often all of these responses are overlapping. Yet, at some point, campaigns are typically called for; counselor educational programs in classrooms, teacher training, student assemblies, posters and banners, parent information and training gatherings, etc. This aspect of any program would also call for clear rules, policies and procedures to be adopted by the school and communicated to the school population at large.

Finally, most programs provide some kind of monitoring processes. Here, teachers, students and parents are asked to keep a specific eye out for bullying activity (they know what to look for because of the informational campaign just discussed). This is especially important in those areas where students have more freedom (at lunch, recess, passing periods, etc.).

For example, the Olweus (1993) anti-bullying program calls for the following actions:

At the School Level:
- Student surveys (assessment)
- Increased student monitoring (assessment/enforcement)
- Whole school awareness informational campaigns, including assemblies, posters, and other communications

At the Classroom Level:
- A curriculum teaching tolerance as well as communication, anger management and conflict resolution skills (awareness/skill training)
- Immediate consequences for aggressive behavior and rewards for inclusive behavior (enforcing policy, bringing change—the requirement is immediate response upon discovery)
- Classroom discussion of incidents when they occur (creating a culture/awareness)

At the Individual Level:
- Serious personal discussion with bully and victim, and their families (awareness, reprimand, training)
- Focused assistance to develop alternative behaviors by both (training/planning)
- Involvement of parents (assessment/enforcement/change)[1]

Here, then, we offer information, provide training, instill incentives (reprimand/reward), make the larger culture aware, and create systems of surveillance. In this, anti-bullying programs can be seen as responding to the five general motivations of school bullying listed above. All of these measures were instituted by Southside K-8 in the bullying incident involving Jake and Matthew. But, the only effect they produced was to lead the bullying of Matthew underground; to more hidden and less obvious venues which were, nonetheless, as destructive as the bump game. To a degree, one might argue that such tactics simply trained Jake to be a more covert, better skilled bully. As I have sat with principals and educators, I have often heard the plea: "We've done all of the activities outlined in anti-bullying programs, but the bullying continues. Are there other answers?" If you recall, in our vignette in Chapter 1, when asked why he continued to bully Matthew, having been instructed and trained, Jake made a simple reply: "Because I like to make him cry." Jake's 'I like' is worth considering and, I will argue, puts a fly in the ointment when considering our traditional anti-bullying responses.

A FLY IN THE OINTMENT: THE 'I LIKE' OF JAKE

Considering the five general motivations which research implicates in bullying activities, we are first led to believe that Jake may have misunderstood that his actions were hurting Matthew. Thus, it was explained to him that Matthew was a person and that his (Jake's) actions were both humiliating and hurtful. It was believed that if one could help Jake 'stand in Matthew's shoes', he would get it; he would understand and stop bullying. But this view does not square with Jake's reason for bullying; i.e., "I like to make him cry." It is apparent that Jake was not only aware of Matthew's tears (and certainly the pain that precipitated them), but that he actually found satisfaction in those tears. If Matthew were to ignore Jake (as he was advised to do), then one imagines that the allure of always knocking Matthew out of the bump game first would fade. It was precisely from the fact the targeting bothered Matthew that the satisfaction was derived. Further, when it was explained to Jake that his actions hurt Matthew, did Jake stop? No, his actions simply became more covert. It seems, then, that the 'I like' of Jake undermines our ability to take seriously the notion that Jake's bullying of Matthew was motivated by a lack of understanding. Instead, it is reasonable to conclude that Jake understood all too well the reaction he sought in Matthew, taking pleasure in the tears of pain exhibited by his victim (Jacobson 2010b).

We are also led to believe that Jake may have lacked the social skills necessary to live well with others. Either Jake struggled with the ability to pick up social cues or, perhaps, he was unable to manage relational aggression. Hence, Jake underwent skill training aimed at helping him to better 'read' those around him, better manage aggression and, thus, live more democratically.

But this view also does not square with Jake's satisfaction derived through Matthew's tears. If Jake was simply relationally incompetent, deeming in some sense that his bullying of Matthew was accidental (i.e., due to missing relational cues or unmanaged aggression), why would he revel in the tears of Matthew? In fact, as indicated in Chapter 2, research clearly indicates that bullies often display an ability to draw others into their activities, exhibiting superior and nuanced social skills (Espelage and Swearer 2003, 365–383; Kaukiainen et al., 1999, 84). Here, one notices the adeptness that Jake displayed in subtly leading 30 classmates in the midst of a bump game to target one student. The skill and subtly necessary for such a process is considerable. Hence, the 'I like' of Jake, and the intentionality that it portrays, undermines our ability to take seriously the notion that his bullying of Matthew was motivated by a lack of skill. Instead, Jake displayed great social dexterity as he intentionally arranged for the tears of Matthew (Jacobson 2010b).

Finally, we are also led to believe that Jake may have simply been a destructive kid; perhaps coming from a bullying family, and was in need of rehabilitation and surveillance. Here Jake is a rule-breaker with a propensity to harm others. Hence, Jake was reprimanded, the bump game was outlawed, a reward and punishment system was enacted, and adults were put on the alert to 'keep an eye on Jake.' While the notion of delinquency may account for Jake's 'I like' (e.g., taking satisfaction in the destruction of another), it yet does not account for Jake's specificity. In other words, why did Jake not show aggression in other ways? He was a popular student, he achieved good grades, and he was respectful of teachers (even liked by teachers) and fellow classmates. Further, why did Jake only target Matthew? If Jake was simply a rule-breaker, a boy out to cause trouble, then could we not assume that he would break other rules or bully other kids? Matthew was Jake's only target that year and the next year, only Trent assumed that role. Again, it seems that the specificity of the 'I like' of Jake undermines our ability to take seriously the notion that his bullying of Matthew was motivated by a fundamental delinquency. Instead, Jake specifically targeted one student, finding satisfaction in the tears of one student, while maintaining strong standing and relationships with the rest of the school community (Jacobson 2010b).

At first glance Jake may seem to be acting out of a lack of understanding, skill deficiency or delinquency, but his 'I like' requires one to question those assumptions. Purposefully, here, I have left out two other possible motivations: inappropriate status acquisition efforts and cultural norming. This is where I will turn next in order to better understand why the good efforts put forward by the staff at Southside K-8 (and those of countless schools across the country) seemed to fall short. I begin with a discussion of the ways that status, student identity and the watching world coalesce to form a foundational element in bullying activity. Here, we'll begin to get a sense of why Jake would risk reprimand and even expulsion in order to continue targeting Matthew; we'll begin to unpack the satisfaction at the heart of Jake's 'I like.'

4 Student Identity Construction
Rethinking the Dominance of Bullying

Pellegrini and Long (2004) echo the research when they argue that bullying activity increases in the middle years (young adolescence). "After all," they contend, "adolescence is a time when youngsters challenge adult roles and values as they search for and construct their own identities" (2004, 108). While bullying certainly is evident in elementary and high school, it seems to peak, or at least become most visible in the middle or junior high years. In fact, some have argued that the ways that we structure schools for this age group may foster bullying behavior.

> A long-standing critique of middle schools and junior high schools, especially in the United States, is that they do not support youngsters' formation of new cooperative, social groups but instead exacerbate fractured social groups by having youngsters attend large schools *which simultaneously stress individual competition, over cooperation* (Eccles et al., 1998). (Pellegrini and Long 2004, 112, emphasis mine)

Here, Pellegrini and Long argue that as students move from smaller, more personal primary schools to larger, less supportive middle schools, well-established social groups are upset. The transition, then, from elementary to middle-school requires the re-establishment of social groups at a time when, according to Pellegrini and Long, "peer relations are particularly important" (2004, 109). "During such transitions," they continue, "aggression is often used in the service of establishing status with peers, in the form of dominance relationships (Strayer, 1980). From this view, bullying is viewed as a deliberate strategy used to attain dominance as youngsters enter a new social group" (2004, 109). Concurring, Gianetti and Sagarese, remind us that, "nearly every young adolescent gets victimized by a peer or group of peers at some time or together during middle school years. . . . The push and pull of social gathering during early adolescence creates outcasts and crises by the dozen" (2001, 90). But, in light of this, why doesn't bullying spike in the transition to high school? And, second, why does the 'upset' of social structures lead to an increase in the dominance that is associated with bullying activities? I will begin by addressing this second question, then turn briefly to the first.

The Satisfaction of another's Tears

In the Southside scenario Jake was asked why he targeted Matthew. His simple reply: because I like to make him cry. As outlined in Chapter 2, the research on school bullying points toward several motivations: a lack of understanding or empathy, poor social skills, etc. In fact, Hoover and Oliver argue that, "*social skills training* was found to be an effective strategy for addressing and combating the factors motivating bullying. In a skills approach, problems are attributed to a lack of knowledge about actions rather than to pathology. Students learn to emit new, more adaptive responses with the help of teachers" (1996, 81 emphasis mine). But, as we discussed in Chapter 3, Jake's 'I like' undermines that theory, at least in part. Jake's bullying of Matthew was not accidental, it was intentional. And, as Pellegrini and Long contend, it 'aimed' at something. What was it about the tears of Matthew that was so satisfying to Jake? More simply I ask: what is the desire to bully a desire for? Of course, because bullying is a complex social phenomenon, that question can be answered in a number of pertinent ways. But I want to stay close to the 'I like' of Jake and consider the exchange of bullying; i.e., what did Jake get, or what was he seeking, in the public humiliation of Matthew? I contend that desire, not social ineptitude is often at the heart of bullying activity. In this chapter I will consider what we're 'doing,' what we are desiring, when we arrange the humiliation of another.

LAUGHTER

Desire is at the heart of most social encounters. We do things for reasons and often those reasons have something to do what desire. Simply, desire means to "wish or long for; to crave; to want" (dictionary.com). *I desire, or want, a sandwich for lunch.* "It is in this simple sense that I employ the word here. Of course, the motivations of desire are difficult, if not impossible, to ferret out. In fact, such desires are not likely to be completely clear even to the one desiring. For example, just because Jake gained satisfaction in the tears of Matthew does not mean that he could articulate where that satisfaction lay" (Jacobson 2009a, 38). But there was something that was exchanged as Jake and the bump crowd roared with laughter, finding Matthew quite hilarious.

Laughing, Fear and a Preferred Self

Adam Phillips in his book *Equals* (2002) takes on the project of democratic relations. At the outset he raises an interesting question. Speaking of the value of the 'helping professions,' here psychoanalysis, Phillips proposes that,

If the best thing we do is look after each other, then the worst thing we do is pretend to look after each other when in fact we are doing something else. One of the many disturbing things about psychoanalysis—as a description of who we are, and as a kind of help—is it shows us why it is often so difficult to tell these things apart. Or rather, it shows us that this distinction, upon which most of our morality depends, is often spurious because we are always likely to be doing both things at once (and several more). Love is not enough, because love is fraught with hatred. It is to what is being taken when we take care of another person that Freud drew our attention. . . . That we can help each other is self-evident (who else can help us if we can't?). What psychoanalysis suggests is that the whole notion of helping people is one of our favourite cover-stories for the moral complexity of exchange. (2002, xi, xii)

In a sense, in Chapter 3 I raise a question: If Jake is doing more than exhibiting social ineptness in his interaction with Matthew, then what is he up to? We have concluded that he may be doing one thing (e.g, targeting a victim he doesn't like or who threatens him), but what if he is doing something else? The complexities of exchange at any level are difficult to discern (e.g., why do we react passive-aggressively with certain people on certain days, but not with other people or on other days?). We face this dilemma even more so with bullying. In essence, Phillips highlights the closeness, and more profoundly the distance, that taints human interchange; typically played out in unequal power encounters. In his exploration of this theme, Phillips entertains two primary questions: "What would have to happen for someone to grow out of the fear of being laughed at? And so, by the same token, what is the fear of being laughed at a fear of?" (2002, 36). What transpired in the laughter that the Southside scene facilitated?

Phillips tells the story of Primo Levi's first impressions of Auschwitz. Levi had had nothing to drink for over four days when he arrived at the camp. Literally, Levi is dying of thirst. Upon arriving at Auschwitz one of the first things Levi notices is a water tap with a sign nearby proclaiming that the water in the tap is 'dirty,' unfit for drinking, and therefore off-limits to the prisoners. Levi sees this as incomprehensible; men dying of thirst, paraded by a water tap, and then told that they cannot drink. Of course, Levi tests the water and, true to the sign's proclamation, finds that the water is, indeed, contaminated. "Levi keeps coming to the conclusion," Phillips explains,

that the only way of explaining this deranged and brutal world he has found himself in is that it is someone's joke; that they are all there being laughed at. And the reason that this is at once grotesque and intelligible as an assumption and an explanation is that when one is being laughed at one is giving someone pleasure. Someone is, as we say, getting pleasure at our expense. (2002, 34–35)

48   *Rethinking School Bullying*

Levi's consternation, according to Phillips, stemmed from the fact that he was giving someone pleasure (i.e., someone must be laughing at the joke of offering men dying of thirst undrinkable water), but at our expense. Moreover, Philips goes on to describe more deeply that in this perceived laughter, something of value is stolen from the target of our laughter.

> When a child asks in the playground, what's so funny, he resents that he is giving someone a pleasure that he has not chosen to give them. Or indeed that something about him provides someone else with a pleasure that diminishes him. When we laugh at someone else we violate, or simply disregard, their preferred image of themselves. (2002, 36)

Our "preferred image," according to Phillips is "that image of ourselves that we believe we are, or hope to be, that image that we seek to convince ourselves and others is true. Of course our preferred images of ourselves often do not line up with reality" (Jacobson 2009a, 39). "The absurd truth that comedy uncovers," Phillips continues,

> . . . is not that really we are undignified and far from important . . . in the larger scheme of things. It is simply that we are always other than what we want to be; that we don't look the same as we look to ourselves. Primo Levi wanted to be what he thought of as a man, but his experience in Auschwitz was that there were other people who didn't share his own description of himself; or indeed of what a person is. For mockery to work, something about a person has to be exposed, usually something they would prefer to conceal from themselves and others because it is at odds with the person they would rather be. (2002, 37)

Here, 'mockery' involves zeroing in on the weaknesses or vulnerabilities or need of another, then exploiting that for our own gain by pointing it out to all. In a sense, is this not reminiscent of Jake's project on the Southside campus? Jake was able to focus in on Matthew's vulnerabilities (e.g., the fact that he cried easily, the fact that he was sensitive, the fact that he didn't have a cadre of powerful friends who would stick up for him, etc.), and by indirectly raising those issues in the bump encounter, he orchestrated the mockery of Matthew. But, how could anyone intentionally do such a thing? Phillips contends that "Children, like adults, have a radar for scarcity, for what [one] might call the unequal distribution of (emotional) wealth. Ridicule, [Phillips suggests], is a fantasy of restoration of status; and mockery is always performed from a position of wished-for privilege" (2002, 38–39). In other words, via the laughter pointed at Matthew, status was accrued by those laughing. Conversely, what was taken from Matthew? "What has been stolen," Phillips argues, is your freedom to supervise, to control the representations of yourself. The other person or people no longer care to protect, or wholly disregard, the images of yourself that you believe you need to sustain you. Humiliation strips the self of its safeguards. (2002, 41)

"There is often a pleasure involved in revealing ourselves to friends, to a close confidant: someone knows me, understands me and accepts me. Such revelation, though, is within our control and is carefully guarded by us. In being laughed at, the locus of control moves from myself to the other in a way that not only exposes me, but also gives the other the pleasure of "viewing me"—the status of standing over me. And as Phillips contends, it is precisely from the fact that the victim hates our laughter that the pleasure is derived. If the victim were not afraid of the laughter of the perpetrator or the crowd, if she were to laugh back, if our laughter did not matter to her, we can imagine that the laughter of the crowd would die down. It would become pointless. The response at being revealed becomes the means of pleasure" (Jacobson 2009a, 39)

On the other hand, Phillips articulates what such laughter might give the ones laughing. He argues that in laughing at another,

> it is the other, not-me, that is mortified. It is, like all cruelty, a calculated not-me experience. I have apparently created a boundary, a distance, between myself and my victim. Indeed, it may be the separateness—the belief that I can instate such a distance—that is the important thing. It is not me who feels this, it is him. So one thing that is so funny at this moment is just how different we are; there is a gulf between us in terms of feeling. My pleasure is as much in your suffering as in my lack of it. What's so funny is that we are both the same kind of creature and yet I can make you worlds apart from me; almost another species, an utterly abject untriumphant one. The shame is now elsewhere, projected or evacuated, as certain psychoanalysts would say. I have rid myself of something unbearable, but I am, as it were, still in touch with it through the medium of pleasure, my sadistic pleasure in your desolation. (Phillips 2002, 42)

Phillips contends that humiliating another is not only aimed at the other. In our anti-bullying programs we often adopt the perspective that the bully has a problem with the victim. But, on Phillips view, that may not be entirely true. Here, the 'laugher's' eyes are focused on himself or herself, seeking to distance some trait, some weakness, their own humiliation, by scapegoating it (i.e., projecting it) on another. In this space we are kept from embracing our own vulnerabilities by distancing ourselves from them and by exposing such weaknesses in another. "Thus, the distance created in laughing at another can, at least in part, also be seen as an attempt to create a preferred sense of self " (Jacobson 2009a, 40). But, "what," Phillips asks, "is the imagined devastation that will occur if the mocker doesn't mock?"

> If he isn't laughing at his victim, if he stops arranging his humiliation, what does he fear might happen? What might they do together? The so-called psychological answer might be he will see too much of himself, too much of something about himself, in his chosen victim. The political answer would be, he would turn democratic. What mockery reveals, in other words, is the emotional terror of democracy. That what is always being ridiculed is our wish to be together, our secret affinity for each other. (2002, 43–44)

"What is laughing at another the fear of? Here, at least in part, laughter rests in the fear that another might have something to say to us, something that might confront our image of ourselves, something that might put us at risk. As it creates boundaries between us and the other, mocking becomes a means of shutting down the dialogue that may threaten our own preferred self-image. Conversely, what is the fear of being laughed at a fear of? It may rest in a fear of discovery, a fear of having the control of our own preferred self-image wrested from our protective vigilance. It becomes a fear that the distance that allows such an image to stay intact might be traversed, not out of our own desire to reveal, but by the violence of another, one intent on enjoying the pleasure of our humiliation" (Jacobson 2009a, 40). Laughter, in Phillip's view, is about creating space for the 'laugher' more than humiliating the target. Here, the bump game provided Jake the space to project his own preferred self-image to the bump crowd, and the larger school population, by laughing. In fact, all who laughed at Matthew, we able to create a place to stand (i.e., status) in the distance they constructed between them and Matthew.

Laughter and a Game of Bump

> As Levi reacted incredulously to the joke of the drinking water, so Matthew was dumbfounded at the pleasure that was involuntarily exacted from him on that Southside playground. Matthew walked away from the bump game and, as the crowd of his peers roared with laughter, was struck with the incomprehensibility being laughed at. The fact that he was giving pleasure to another was understandable, but this pleasure was stolen from him, beyond his control, thus humiliating. Phillips helps us consider that the ridicule of bullying, the laughter on that Southside playground, was situated in the establishment of a preferred image on the part of the bully through the destruction (or revelation) of the preferred image of another, the victim. As Matthew was revealed, the preferred image of Jake (powerful, privileged and in control) was

displayed for all to see. In essence, "a self" was projected in the destruction of another. (Jacobson 2009a, 40–41)

Sometimes it's hard for us to comprehend the cruelty involved in the public humiliation of another. Phillips suggests at least one motivation for such activities. He argues that "Ridicule . . . is a fantasy of restoration of status; and mockery is always performed from a position of wished-for privilege" (2002, 38–39). Pellegrini and Long argue that bullying "is a specific form of aggression and one that is used deliberately to secure resources. Bullying seems to be used as a way in which boys gain and maintain dominance status with peers" (2004, 109–110). Of course, through the never-ending power imbalances between humans, it is not only boys who seek status through dominance; research shows that girls are just as active in such processes. "Phillips posits that the pleasure of laughing at another is connected with desire, i.e., "wished for privilege." Pellegrini and Long argue that the aggression inherent in bullying is used deliberately, it is intentionality fostered by desire. More than simple reaction, bullying from these viewpoints becomes an intentional means to some end based in some desire; specifically the desire to maintain dominance status with peers. As Phillips suggests, this desire is connected with scarcity, with some emotional commodity that laughing at another secures" (Jacobson 2009a, 41).

Further, as outlined in Chapter 2, bullying is primarily a social event; over 85 percent of bullying episodes involve peers knowing, watching, or participating. The bump game is a prime example. If Jake simply took joy in dominating Matthew, why not beat him up (physically or verbally) in a bathroom stall or on a hidden corner of the playground? Instead, Jake orchestrated the exposure of Matthew's weakness before thirty of the school's 'who's who' in the most popular game on campus. It is the fact that the humiliation mattered to Matthew that allowed the bullying to work; but, more so, it was the fact that it mattered to the thirty students who watched that made it satisfying. Here, we begin to understand Jake's "I like." To gain status always means to gain status *with* others. Jake's status, linked to his preferred image projected in his domination of Matthew, was secured in the smiles, whispers, and high-fives of his classmates. But, it wasn't just Jake who gained status through this public humiliation of Matthew. "Indeed, all who watched and participated gained in the status of rising above Matthew and wresting from him his own preferred image of himself. The laughter of the bump crowd became effective—lowering the status of Matthew and concurrently raising the status of those who laughed (i.e., "at least *I'm* not as pathetic as Matthew!")—because that laughter held currency for all involved" (Jacobson 2009a, 42). Hence, the satisfaction of bullying comes not only from gaining status for the bully, but from his/her 'benevolence' in securing status for all of those watching as well.

Phillips argues that laughing at another creates space between the weakness we see in them and ourselves. In this distance we are given a 'place to stand' that is valued by others and, thus, satisfying to ourselves. But, one might ask, why did Jake need to continue to bully Matthew even after his status was secured with the bump crowd. Everyone knew Jake was 'the better man'; in fact the entire campus was aware of the demise of Matthew, making the sting deeper for Matthew and the glory greater for Jake. And why, the next year, was that desire to humiliate another (if, indeed, it was directed toward securing dominance status with peers) aimed at a new target? In other words, why might such quests for status through dominance become insatiable?

BEING SOMEONE THROUGH DOMINANCE

How is it that we gain our sense of identity? Do we just look in the mirror and come up with a sense of who we are on our own? And, even more vexing, how might the domination involved in bullying be a part of Jake's 'identity-construction' process? Jessica Benjamin, in *The Bonds of Love: Psychoanalysis, Feminism and the Problem of Domination* (1988), takes on a pertinent project. She is interested primarily in male/female relations, seeking to understand what domination and submission 'gives' to the participants. In other words, considering common gender roles, she wonders what men 'get' out of dominating women and, more controversially, what women 'get' out of being dominating. Here, similar to my project, she is interested in the exchange of domination.

Benjamin argues that humans have a basic need to recognize and be recognized by other human beings. In this she finds the importance of reciprocity in relationships; i.e., a balance between assertion and recognition. In this process, she argues, identity gets constructed. This begins early with parent-child relationships; parents asserting/responding to the child, giving the child a sense of place, connection, and meaning. But, Benjamin would argue, the child also pushes back (e.g., he cries, she smiles, etc.), affirming the parent as provider, parent, etc. On Benjamin's view, this give and take, assertion and recognition, is at the heart of human identity construction. Benjamin argues that "domination and submission result from a breakdown of the necessary tension between self-assertion and mutual recognition that allows self and other to meet as sovereign equals" (1988, 12). Maintaining the "assumption that we are fundamentally social beings" (1988, 17), Benjamin argues that the "individual grows in and through the relationship to other subjects" (1988, 19–20). It is interesting to note that peer relationships become paramount in the middle school experience at the same time when young adolescents are working to create identity individuated from family life and, as research tells us, bullying activity also spikes in the middle school years. I will consider this reality a bit more shortly.

Using Each Other

Seeking to understand male dominance of females, Benjamin outlines the process of differentiation used by boys and girls in relation to the mother. Briefly, she argues that cultural norms impact mother-child relationships, influencing boys to move toward creating identity through differentiation from the mother, while directing girls toward a pathway of identification with the mother.[1] Of course, such a notion is controversial, but my intent is not to ferret out the nuances of mother/father relations in child psychic development. Instead, I'm interested in the notion of 'splitting' that Benjamin raises in this process. Here one, typically the male, asserts while the other, usually the female, is asserted upon (as the boy seeks for form identity through independence and the girls through identification). For Benjamin this is problematic because she believes that it is only through the process of assertion/recognition that identity can be established. "Benjamin argues that 'the two central elements of recognition—being like and being distinct—are split apart,' and that this splitting (one dominating as subject, the other dominated as object) leaves both without any real subjectivity. The male as dominator leaves no room for anyone to "push back," thus confirming (or recognizing) his own subjectivity. The other here becomes an object, not a subject offering recognition. Alternatively, the female, as she is dominated, loses her own subjectivity, and thus is no longer available to offer recognition (since she becomes only a reflection of her dominator), nor to receive recognition (since she has become only a concrete object in this dynamic)" (Jacobson 2009a, 44).

To some degree, we might simply imagine in this process of assertion and recognition that humans simply serve as mirrors for each other. When we look at a mirror, it mimics back to us what we look like, thus giving us a sense of ourselves. This understanding misses the deeper intent of Benjamin's argument. "The mother cannot (and should not) be a mirror;" Benjamin contends, "she must not merely reflect back what the child asserts; she must embody something of the not-me; she must be an independent other who responds in her different way" (1988, 24). According to Benjamin, domination results when this assertion/recognition process is separated between two people; again, for her, between male and female. "Hence, when the mother is seen as object (females as those who are asserted upon) and father is seen a subject (males as those who assert upon) domination results" (Jacobson 2009a, 44). Here, I'm interested in the give and take between a bully and a victim. Of course, domination is situated in relationship were one asserts and one is asserted upon, but more foundationally in this process of splitting we create a scenario where such domination becomes insatiable; never really satisfying the aim of such domination. In other words, if I am 'using' domination of another to gain a sense of self, and yet a sense of self only comes through reciprocal relationships, then what I am looking for is never realized. Here are clues to why Jake continued to target Matthew again and again and why the next year he felt the need to target Trent as well. At the heart of this process is the notion of 'object usage.'

Using the Other

Benjamin contends that, rather than simply 'seeing ourselves' in others, we engage in a process of assertion and recognition, using those around us to create a sense of who we are. In a sense, we *use* the other to create a sense of self. Let me illustrate what this 'use' may entail. Imagine for a minute that I am an outstanding rock guitarist. Imagine further that I have just finished a mind-blowing guitar solo with my band in front of 100,000 fans at a new world class outdoor venue. During this 20 minute solo, I played with the skill of Hendrix and Clapton, concluding the mind-blowing display with stage pyrotechnics that would make any public New Year's display jealous. Finally, imagine at the end of that solo, as the smoke cleared, the crowd remained absolutely silent. No response what-so-ever. This could be, of course, because they were so overwhelmed by the sheer beauty of my playing (i.e., leaving them speechless). But, in this case, the silence signaled the fact that they were wholly unimpressed by my performance. What is my reaction? I must be a terrible guitar player or at best, it was a terrible solo!

In fact, to 'know' that I am an outstanding musician I need the crowd to roar with pleasure. I need them to buy my CDs, or download my music, or buy tickets to my concerts in order to measure my talent. I don't need the crowd to play guitars back to me (i.e., mirror what I'm doing). Instead, I need to know that they were impacted by my assertion (i.e., my playing) and, thus, their response is linked to my guitar-playing, but appropriately different (i.e., I need them to clap, to cheer, to rave!). Is this not how we often measure our performance or abilities? If I am a teacher and my students continually perform poorly on standardized tests, then I must be a poor teacher. But, if struggling students in a class that I have inherited in the fall, ace the test in the spring, I certainly must be a great teacher. I may even be nominated for teacher of the year! If I write a book and no one buys it, it must be a subpar book and I must be a poor author. But, if I write my first book and it sells a million copies, then I am a sensational writer. This is not meant to argue the nuances of merit and what art is appreciated or not. Instead, the point I make here is that we need the 'reactions' of others in order to build a sense of who we are (e.g., I solo on my guitar, you clap wildly, I must be a good guitar player). Here, my identity (i.e., my own sense of who I am) is dependent on those around me (i.e., how they react to me, what they say about me, how they speak to me, what they think of me). On this view, we 'use' each other to build identity. Of course, this process of assertion and recognition is ongoing throughout our lives. Certainly, the longer we live the greater sense of who we are is developed; but that sense of identity is always fluid and always social. In fact, it makes sense that for middle schoolers, at the precise age when research tells us that identity construction is at its height (moving from childhood to adulthood), social relationships also become extremely important. One might argue that as the need to establish identity for middle schoolers spikes, so does the need to 'use' peers to establish that sense of self. Middle-schoolers 'play their guitars' for each other, looking for the reaction of peers to confirm who they are becoming.

Important to this discussion is the notion of 'object destruction.' Emmanuel Ghent, in his article *Masochism, Submission, and Surrender* (1990) defines the process of object usage in greater detail (for a critique of "object usage" see McNay 1992, 84). He contends that, "the object if it is to be used, must necessarily be real in the sense of being part of shared reality" (1990, 123). In other words, there needs to be a concrete other (i.e., a real person) who, in the give and take of relations, is used to confirm the identity. For example, it's not enough for me to fantasize that the crowd loves my guitar playing (we've all done this!); I need an actual audience to clap. In psychoanalytic terms, when we 'assert' we are seeking to 'destroy' the other. This sounds harsh, but object destruction simply implies pushing against another. If they are able or willing to push back, thus not destroyed by our assertion, then we are 'recognized.' "In a child's development," argues Benjamin, "the initial destruction can be seen simply as part of assertion: the desire to affect (negate) others, to be recognized. When destruction fails [i.e., the other is not allowed, or for some reason, doesn't push back], the aggression goes inside and fuels the sense of omnipotence" (1988, 69). This is crucial to our understanding of the insatiability of bullying: "If the other is destroyed—through domination—then that other cannot assert back, or confirm a sense of self. If the other survives (i.e., asserts back), a sense of self now finds concrete confirmation" (Jacobson 2009a, 45).

But, what does destruction, or non-survival, look like? "The varieties of non-survival," writes Ghent, "include retaliation, withdrawal, defensiveness in any of its forms, . . . and finally, a kind of crumbling, in the sense of its losing one's capacity to function adequately as a mother, or in the analytic setting, as an analyst" (1990, 123). Thus, when we assert and another is destroyed, the other becomes incapable of response. Remember, here, that reciprocity is at the heart of identity confirmation; thus, when the other is destroyed by our assertion, that assertion cannot be reciprocated. This may take place because the 'victim' crumbles or withdraws on her own accord, or it may, in the case of a sadist, happen because the 'victim' is not allowed to reciprocate. The 'masochist' (the one who in Benjamin's terms takes up a submissive, dominated role) may be shaped when a parent or other powerful figure impinges upon them. This 'authoritarian' parent, as we discussed in Chapter 2, is implicated in the research as one possible source in the fostering of bullying tendencies. On the other hand, according to Ghent, the sadist (the one who in Benjamin's terms takes up an omnipotent, dominating role) may be formed by a parent who continually crumbles (or is destroyed) by the child. In this situation the parent is destroyed through,

> retaliation, defensiveness, negativity or [a] crumbling of her or his effectiveness. In either case, the triple misfortune is that the subjective object never becomes real but remains a bundle of projections, and externality is not discovered; as a corollary the subject is now made to feel that he or she is destructive; and finally, fear and hatred of the other develops, and with them, characterological destructiveness comes into being. In short we have the setting for the development of sadism, the need to aggressively control the other as a perversion of object usage, much as we have seen in masochism as a perversion of surrender. (Ghent 1990, 124)

Ghent imagines who this plays on in family dynamics.[2] If as the child asserts upon the parent, the parent crumbles or withdraws, the reciprocity needed to confirm the child's sense of self is eclipsed. Thus, the child continues to assert, looking for confirmation (a parent or other who will assert back), but in the crumbling, or destruction of the other, the child's need to be confirmed continues to be unmet. Ghent concludes that the will to dominate another, thus, becomes "a derivative of the wish to discover the reality of the other, and thereby truly experience the self" (1990, 125). In the act of domination, the other is not allowed to reciprocate and is thus destroyed. And, as Benjamin asserts above, when one only dominates, a growing sense of omnipotence develops, further precluding the reciprocity needed to satisfy what the dominator is looking for in the first place.

"Establishing myself," Benjamin argues, "means winning the recognition of the other, and this, in turn, means I must finally acknowledge the other as existing for himself and not just for me" (1988 36). In order for my own sense of self to be confirmed, it is crucial that the other is affected by my assertion "so that I know that I exist—but not completely destroyed, so that I know he also exists" (1988, 38). Here, if I play my guitar and the crowd does nothing, or storms out, the need to continue to play for others to find out if I'm any good can become compulsive. Likewise, if I play and force the audience to clap (i.e., they have no choice but to submit to my demand), I am still left with the same compulsion to play for other audiences because my playing has yet to be confirmed. It is only through playing for an audience and receiving their honest response that I can begin to construct a sense of myself as a guitar player.

"A sense of self, then, is embroiled in the use and destruction of another, but it is only as the other presses back (i.e., is not destroyed) that that sense of self is truly confirmed. In the splitting outlined by Benjamin such mutuality is foregone, thus denying self-confirmation. Hence, as a self is attempted to be confirmed in the omnipotence inherent in such splitting, the domination at work becomes insatiable, since the self always eludes confirmation in such non-mutual relations" (Jacobson 2009a, 48).

Moving from Accident to Intention

I argue, here, that rather than accidental (skill deficiency, and in ability to control aggression, or even a lack of understanding), bullying is intentional. This is certainly born out in the research. I also argue that as the majority of all bullying encounters are public encounters, the social nature of bullying is salient. Further, the research bears out that bullying is typically aimed at establishing status dominance (status through dominance) by the bully. As I have outlined in this chapter, status is always status *with* others (or in the eyes of others). If this is true, then we are left with the understanding that a fundamental component of bullying is focused in creating a preferred sense of identity in the eyes of a watching crowd. Bullying, here, is a practice of public identity construction. Yet, if identity can only be established in reciprocity (i.e., I play the guitar and you clap), then in relations of domination (i.e., I play the guitar louder and louder without any response) the very identity we seek becomes elusive. Here, bullying becomes insatiable in its attempt to establish the self through domination, instead of through the assertion and response interaction at the heart of identity confirmation. The omnipotence of the bully leaves him or her without the confirmation necessary to gain the sense of identity that is at the heart of their project.

"Phillips, Benjamin and Ghent help us envision the bump game as a tool—an ill-fated attempt employing domination and distancing—used by students to gain subjectivity. The quest for domination involved in the bullying relationship can be seen as a failed quest for such subjectivity, for status, seeking to secure a place for the self to stand. In this domination the bullies, seeking to find someone to recognize them, find only an object that, laughing at, they slowly destroy. And in destroying Matthew, they are left searching for someone else to recognize their own subjectivity—thus, picking a new target (Trent) when the current target becomes unavailable" (Jacobson 2009a, 48).

BULLYING, DESIRE, AND STATUS

Benjamin and Ghent find that reciprocity, the give and take with another, is at the root of identity construction (i.e., we become "selves" socially). Both Benjamin and Ghent also argue that dominance often becomes a means of attempted identity construction. In other words, dominating another (and doing so publicly in a bullying situation), means that I am better; I am higher. This dominance aims at securing status in the eyes of onlookers. We witness this "giving" or "taking" of status in the high-fives and backslapping and knowing smiles of those who participated in the demise of Matthew on that Southside playground. Here bullying is not just about creating a pecking order, but is based upon the notion that that pecking order tells the world and ourselves who we are. But, as Benjamin argues, when we seek to establish identity through dominance, we indeed eclipse the possibility of the reciprocity which is necessary for such identity construction.

This brings me back to my first question posed at the outset of this chapter: why does bullying activity spike in middle school? The obvious answer, articulated by Pellegrini and Long above, is that middle school is a point of significant change for young adolescents. This is certainly true as students transition from smaller, local community elementary schools (with the same teacher/classmates throughout the day), to larger, comprehensive middle and junior high schools (transitioning through periods with different teachers, sets of peers and expectations). This transition upsets the normal social structures, requiring students to re-socialize peer groups and pecking orders. But, in some sense, the transition to high school involves very similar processes. Why don't we see another increase in bullying activity at that point?

If, as I have suggested, a fundamental aspect of bullying involves attempted identity construction, then one would expect a burgeoning of such activities in the middle school years. It is in these years that children begin the transition from childhood to adulthood; not only academically, but cognitively, developmentally, physically, hormonally, and socially. In these transitions, according to Pellegrini and Long, middle-schoolers are hard at work searching for and constructing their own identities. As Brown and Knowles contend, "Every young adolescent at some time from sixth through eighth grade experiences questions about his or her place in the social milieu" (2007, 37). "Despite interest in conforming and belonging to a social group," Brown and Knowles continue, "young adolescents still want individuality. The need for confirmation by a social group is really a need for personal validation. . . . The desire for peer approval is an extension of the desire to have their personal choices validated" (2007, 53, 43). In these middle years students begin a season of significant transformation brought on by hormonal changes which affect the way they think, their bodies, their social connections, as well as their emotional well-being. "Young adolescence," conclude Brown and Knowles, "brings with it life's first identity crisis, in which students attempt to project an image consistent with the inner self, which they hope will be accepted by others who make up their world" (2007, 65); i.e., middle-schoolers are looking for themselves in the eyes of their peers.

Research tells us that bullying activity spikes during the middle school years. Why might that be? In the transition from childhood to adulthood middle school students begin in an overt way to wrestle with their own identity. And, if as I have suggested, identity construction is always a social process (we find status *with* others), then we would expect social realities to become more important at those points of identity transition. It is in the give and take (reciprocity) of those interactions that middle-schoolers work to develop a sense of self. Here, is fertile ground for public domination to become a meaningful pathway to preferred status within the schools. Bullying in middle school becomes a pathway to rise above another publicly, to look strong, to project a preferred image to peers at the very point when identity is most fluid (i.e., when we are shifting from childhood—where we find much of our identity with our families, to young adulthood when we learn to be our own person). Here, in the milieu of middle school culture, bullying becomes a viable means of identity construction by gaining status in the eyes of our peers through the public domination of a weaker classmate.

CONCLUSION

If, as I have argued, bullying activity is foundationally an attempt at self-construction, a social activity seeking to establish a preferred self-image with others, and, thus, a meaningful *place to stand*, then any amount of skill-based training will likely fall flat. If Jake used dominance to create identity in the eyes of his peers, then teaching him to be more in control of his aggression misses the point; the point is, he already is in control of that aggression, employing it specifically and skillfully toward the demise of another in who's destruction all can bask. Further, asking Jake to stop is like asking Primo Levi to not drink water from an open tap. When Jake considered what was at stake (being punished or even expelled compared with finding a meaningful identity with peers in the transition from childhood to adulthood), the reprimand of an adult surely paled in comparison. As Matthew was destroyed, all of those involved gained a sense of status. But, according to Phillips, Ghent, and Benjamin, "selves" can only be created as the "other" pushes back. Thus, bullying, despite our rules, training, and surveillance becomes insatiable.

"Jake was laughing. The bump crowd was roaring. And Matthew was crying. On that Southside playground, as observed by students and teachers alike, we witness a lesson in attempted self-construction, one that disallows the reciprocity necessary for a sense of self to emerge" (Jacobson 2009a, 50). But why, one might ask, does dominance become the avenue of choice in this work? In other words, why does dominance bring status? Why not kindness, or big feet, or being last in the 50 meter dash? When Jake organized the bump game, inviting in other students, when he publicly humiliated Matthew, it worked. What I mean, is that the pathway of dominance and public humiliation became a pathway toward status in the eyes of the watching crowd on that playground. How, we might ask, do such displays of dominance strike a chord in the school setting?

5 Dominance and Schooling
Parallel Narratives from the Same Cloth

As I think back to my high school experience only a handful of students come to mind. I'd say that out of a total population of around 1,200 students, about 100 had some sort of campus-wide notoriety. There was Jim Monde. He was tall, affable, the high scorer on the basketball team, and had a great sense of humor. Everyone knew Jim. Then, there was Deena Foss. She was a Principal's daughter, beautiful and kind. She also had great hair! Speaking of hair, there was Marvin Becker. Marvin played sports, but certainly wasn't a star. Though somewhat soft spoken, he was well liked because of his 'easy manner.' He dressed well and, most importantly, he had outstanding, perfectly-feathered hair. Everyone knew Marvin Becket. Finally, there was Jerry Pass. He was the class clown; a cut-up, but well-liked and funny. Every school has its cast of notables; those students who are widely known and liked. But, here's the rub. Those 100 needed the other 1100 to be somebody. In other words, it was the recognition of the other 1,100 and the fact that the other 1100 weren't one of the 100 that allowed the notoriety of the 100 to be meaningful. Drawing on our example in Chapter 4, if everyone was a star guitar player, then all would cease to be a star. The fact that there are ordinary guitar players allows 'star' guitar players to stand out. Notoriety is similar; popular cliques exist because they are exclusive (i.e., they stand apart from everyone else). But, I'm interested in the stories that allow some students to rise above, to be special, and others to be ordinary. In other words, how does a student become someone in the school setting? More pointedly, I wonder how the 'ideal' students (e.g., Jim Monde, Deena Foss, Marvin Becker, etc.) motivate others to be like them and how that plays out in schools. In this chapter I will focus on the pathways of status and identity that are salient in schools; pathways that I will argue mirror the very bullying behavior that we distain. More pointedly I ask: how does a bully show up in the school setting?

DISCIPLINARIAN TRAINING

The million dollar question: What factors motivated Jake to take up bullying at Southside K-8? Was he a troubled kid from a distant or domineering home? Was he a bit of sadist; enjoying the pain of others? Did he simply not have the cultural inhibitions instilled socially to curb any inclinations to publicly humiliate a classmate? As outlined in Chapter 2, to some degree research indicates the 'delinquency' of the bully. The bully is seen as an individual who takes pleasure in the pain of others ('I like to make him cry'), or someone who is anti-social or might be regarded as a rule-breaker. The intentionality involved in bullying bolsters this notion of a bully who desires to harm a classmate because of intolerance or some other salient motivation. But, a bully is seen as a student who not only seeks to harm a classmate, but one who does so publicly, disrupting the friendship circles and status of the victim in significant ways. A bully intentionally takes advantage of a weaker classmate. Here, bullies become problem students who must be disciplined, trained and reinstated to healthy and appropriate social interaction. This is a staple understanding in most anti-bullying responses.

From such assumptions, and quite understandably, most anti-bullying strategies involve some focus on 'rehabilitation.' As indicated in Chapter 2, this includes a number of facets: reprimand (e.g., stern talks, behavioral expectations tied to clear rewards and punishments); reward (e.g., acknowledgement of appropriate behavior through incentives and/or public recognition) aimed at applying pressure to change motivation; disciplinary training (e.g., anger management or social skills training, teacher modeling, behavioral contracting) aimed at training behavior; and surveillance (adult supervisors, teachers, peer monitoring and self-monitoring) aimed at long term transformation through accountability and consequence. In this vein, Jake and his accomplices were called to the principal's office and reprimanded, the bump game was outlawed, Jake and his friends underwent anger management and empathy building skill programs, peers were drawn in to put pressure on bullies and all were watched (Jake and Matthew) as teachers and recess personnel were notified. It was assumed that these measures would change, or rehabilitate, Jake's propensity to publicly humiliate a classmate. These are the typical elements that come to mind when we consider processes of moral education. But in the Southside story, even after reprimand, training, and surveillance, Jake did not stop. In fact, they motivated him to 'improve his technique'; working to bully Matthew in ways that were visible to peers, but hidden from adults. In some sense, one might argue that the anti-bullying process in place actually trained Jake to be a better bully. Of course, as I argued in the last chapter that if, indeed, Jake's status was on the line, then he would easily endure reprimands in order to maintain his preferred standing with his peers. But, one might ask, why is dominance esteemed in the school setting in the first place? Using the work of Michel Foucault, specifically as he explicates disciplinary training, I want to consider the ways we motivate students to be better; specifically paying attention to the 'training' we employ within schools. I begin, of all places, with Foucault's analysis of prisons and their project of rehabilitation.[1]

Discipline and Punish

> The chief function of the disciplinary power is to 'train' . . . Instead of bending all its subjects into a single uniform mass, it separates, analyses, differentiates, carries its procedures of decomposition to the point of necessary and sufficient single units. . . . Discipline 'makes' individuals; it is the specific technique of a power that regards individuals both as objects and as instruments of its exercise. (Foucault 1995, 170)

In *Discipline and Punish* (1995), Foucault undertakes an anthropology of punishment and so-called rehabilitation. More deeply, in all of his work, Foucault is interested in the ways subjects (i.e., identities) get narrated or construed through the discourses and practices that surround us. But, of course, coming from a poststructuralist view, Foucault would argue that subjects are always being narrated (being shaped by their cultures), as well as narrating (shaping their worlds). For example, on a micro level all of us have been 'shaped' by our families (what was said to us as well as the traditions or norms that were lived out—e.g., holiday traditions, summer vacations, etc.). But, the narration, or shaping, was not a one-way street. We also influenced our families by our own personalities, learning, and experiences. This 'narration,' specifically as it applies to prisons and rehabilitation is the subject of Foucault's inquiry.

In earlier days, contends Foucault, punishment was meted out as a spectacle for all to see. "Public torture and execution must be spectacular," writes Foucault, "it must be seen by all almost as [the law's] triumph. The very excess of the violence employed is one of the elements of its glory" (1995, 34). According to Foucault, initially punishment in the form of public execution was to highlight "the dissymmetry between the subject who has dared to violate the law and the all-powerful sovereign who displays his strength" (1995, 48–49). Here punishment was focused on "revealing the power of the monarch and thus extending his iron fist over the larger population" (Jacobson 2010a, 262). But over time a shift occurred; illegal activity was not simply a crime against the king, but against society itself. Foucault contends that "the right to punish . . . shifted from the vengeance of the sovereign to the defence [sic] of society" (1995, 90). Foucault asserts that, "punishment, initially focused upon revenge (i.e., an eye for an eye) moved toward a restriction of rights, then to an agenda of rehabilitation. More than a simple act, crime became focused on the criminal, an obsession with intent, propensity to harm, and character" (Jacobson 2010a, 263). Consider current crime narratives (whether a school shooting or violence of any kind); one of the first questions we ask is, "why?" In bullying, why did the bully bully? Why did s/he target the victim? Here, understanding intent allows us to begin to imagine rehabilitation. Punishment became aimed not at revenge or paying the offender back, but toward transformation of character. "Punishment . . . will be an art of effects," Foucault writes, "one must punish exactly enough to prevent repetition" (1995, 93). The work of prisons became focused on training and rehabilitation as the means of prevention.

As a means of rehabilitation and training the *panoptic* system was proposed. This system involved constructing cells around a central surveillance tower. Key to this system was the notion that every space, even open non-barred areas were constructed so that they could always be seen from the tower (or some other clear vantage point). Surveillance in such a system is complete, penetrating and one-sided. "Each individual," explains Foucault,

> in his place, is securely confined to a cell from which he is seen from the front by the supervisor; but the side walls prevent him from coming into contact with his companions. He is seen, but he does not see; he is the object of information, never a subject in communication. (1995, 200)

The key to the panoptic system is that all behavior would take place under the "watchful eye." "In this training multiple aspects of life—behavior, time, speech, body, activity, sexuality—are observed and controlled. Here, the prisoner learns to watch himself, but, Foucault would argue, so do others as well (e.g., wardens, guards, etc.). The system norms all within its purview" (Jacobson 2010a, 263). The idea, here, is that through surveillance we can transform a delinquent into a better citizen. How? Through regimes of watching, training, disciplining, and rewarding. If one is constantly in view of authority, then we are not only watched, but we learn to watch ourselves. In some sense this is a behaviorialistic view of moral transformation. We are trained by being watched and, over time, we form new habits. This becomes a difficult proposition in regards to bullying for at least a couple reasons. First, Simmons argues that we can directly watch two students while bullying is taking place and yet not see it. We simply can't be close enough to monitor every conversation, every look, or every nuanced stance. Bullying isn't always overtly physical and, thus we can't always see it. Here, cyber bullying becomes even more problematic when we consider regimes of training and surveillance. The second problematic issue that arises from the panoptic system, involves the notion that such systems tend to focus on behavior more than heart. Certainly there is a motivation to avoid punishment, but in the case of bullying, does constant surveillance help a bully no longer *want* to bully? Even more foundationally, Foucault brings up a third problematic reality regarding this system. This system of surveillance and punishment or reward was thought to be a means of 'knowing' the criminal and, thus, rehabilitating her more effectively. But in his anthropology of the prison system, Foucault comes to the conclusion that "prisons do not diminish the crime rate: they can be extended, multiplied or transformed, the quantity of crime and criminals remains stable or, worse, increases" (1995, 265). Here I am reminded of the Washington State University study (2008), which found that even after laws and policies were on the books, bullying continued at similar levels. Unfortunately, as indicated in Chapter

2, anti-bullying programs are uneven at best in their effectiveness. When it comes to bullying, regimes of reprimand and surveillance do not work as well as we often hope they would for a number of reasons. Foucault provocatively argues that rather than rehabilitating the criminal, prisons become a means of norming the larger population.[2] But, for our purposes, I am interested in the methodologies of narration employed by such disciplinary or training systems. Here I come to the important conception of what Foucault calls "dividing practices."

Dividing Practices

In *Discipline and Punish*, Foucault details the training methods employed by prisons (though he expands this to include the training used in the military as well as in schools). Primarily such training is exacted through regimes of individuation. Foucault contends that

> At the beginning of the seventeenth century Walhausen spoke of "strict discipline" as an art of correct training. . . . Instead of bending all its subjects into a single, uniform mass, it separates, analyzes, differentiates, carries its procedures of decomposition to the point of necessary and sufficient single units. It "trains" the moving, confused, useless multitudes of bodies and forces into a multiplicity of individual elements—small, separate cells; organizes autonomies; genetic identities and continuities; combinatory segments. Discipline "makes" individuals; it is the specific technique of a power that regards individuals both as objects and as instruments of its exercise." (1995, 170)

Training became dependent upon what Foucault calls "dividing practices," which both separate and rank those being trained in order to motivate rehabilitation (i.e., training aimed at transformation). This individuation is brought to bear in different ways. First, dividing practices break down specific human bodies by focusing training on specific components of the human body.

> What was so new, in these projects of docility that interested the eighteenth century so much? . . . To begin with there was the scale of the control: it was a question not of treating the body, en masse, 'wholesale', as if it were an indissociable unity, but of working it 'retail', individually; of exercising upon it a subtle coercion, of obtaining holds upon it at the level of the mechanism itself—movements, gestures, attitudes, rapidity: an infinitesimal power over the active body, (Foucault 1995, 136–137)

Here discipline, through dividing practices, sought to recreate humans that could be "subjected, used, transformed and improved" (Foucault 1995,

136). The first component of such 'dividing practices' involves dividing the individual body into its component parts. Hence, in schools, we might train the hand in penmanship, the eye in literacy, the mind in writing, and the mouth in speech. Focusing on each part of the body, exacting perfection in these separate domains, allows us to then bring them back together; for example, having trained a student to prepare, write, and give a speech in class. The body is seen in its separate parts (hands, feet, ears, etc.) and these are, "then taken up separately and subjected to a precise and calculated training. The aim is control and efficiency of operation both for the part and the whole" (Dreyfus and Rabinow 1983, 153).

Through breaking the soldier into specific 'parts' specific emphasis could be brought to bear with the understanding that when the 'trained' part were brought together the end result would be a well-disciplined whole. This method, according to Foucault, not only was used in prisons, but came to be employed in all kinds of trainings (e.g., schools, the military, professions with specific skill sets, etc.) The disciplines,

> notably the army and the schools—were quietly developing techniques and tactics to treat human beings as objects to be molded, not subjects to be heard or signs to be circulated and read. (Dreyfus and Rabinow 1983, 154)

The panopticon was central to this project of separation. According to Foucault, the prisoner became 'the object of information, never a subject in communication' (Foucault 1995, 200). Information becomes foundational in the process of training. In this 'one way' view of training, understanding the subject of our discipline (the specific prisoner, solider or student) allows us to develop specific techniques of molding and surveillance necessary for transformation. These 'dividing practices' which were the heart of training certainly involved the body (i.e., training the hand for better penmanship), but also involved the control time and movement. Such training, according to Foucault,

> implies an uninterrupted, constant coercion, supervising the processes of the activity rather than its result and it is exercised according to a codification that partitions as closely as possible time, space, movement. These methods, which made possible the meticulous control of the operations of the body, which assured the constant subjection of its forces and imposed upon them a relation of docility-utility, might be called 'disciplines.' (1995, 137)[3]

But, these dividing practices were not only to be focused on the specific body parts of the individual being training; they also brought individuation to the population at large. While the focus on training a hand or an eye brings up important questions regarding the aims of schooling, this second aspect of the 'dividing practices' allow an important point of analysis in light of the pathways school bullying follows. According to Foucault, training not only seeks to divide individual humans into component parts upon which to bring pressure to bear, but this training also separates or divides one human from another to foster motivation. Normalization becomes a catalyst for rehabilitation, but normalization only works to motivate if it is connected with comparison and hierarchy. "Each individual has a place and each place has its individual," writes Foucault (1995, 143). This individuation, one student from another, is central to the training process.

> The art of punishing in the regime of disciplinary power, is aimed neither at expiation, nor even precisely at repression. It brings five quite distinct operations into play: it refers individual actions to a whole that is at once a field of comparison, a space of differentiation, and the principle of a rule to be followed. It differentiates individuals from one another in terms of the following overall rule, that the rule be made to function as a minimal threshold, as an average to be respected, or as an optimum toward which one must move. It measures in quantitative terms and hierarchizes in terms of value the abilities, the level, the "nature" of individuals. It introduces through this "value-giving" measure, the constraint of a conformity that must be achieved. Lastly, it traces the limit that will define difference in relation to all other differences, the external frontier of the abnormal . . . The perpetual penalty that traverses all points and supervises every instant in the disciplinary institutions compares, differentiates, hierarchizes, homogenizes, excludes. In short, it *normalizes*. (Foucault 1995, 182–183).

Here, training aimed at shaping individuals focuses not only on breaking students down into their individual components, but dividing and organizing them from each other within the system via comparison.[4] For example, students are directed toward the goal of the ideal student, then measured against each other to see who is closer to the ideal. I often ask students in my education courses to tell me about the ideal student; what are the characteristics of such a student? The list inevitably contains qualities such as: someone who works hard, someone who sits quietly, someone who 'gets it' when I teach, someone who is respectful, someone who is interested in the subject manner and engaged in learning, someone who participates (neither dominating, nor disappearing from class discussions), someone whose parents are involved in the right ways (i.e., not hovering, but not absent), someone who does their homework and shows improvement, someone who performs well on assessments, is a good test-taker, is athletic, has lots of friends, dresses appropriately, listens attentively, follows directions, who is positive, caring, pleasant, clean, funny, punctual, etc. Then, I ask my students to list the qualities of a non-ideal students: someone who struggles academically or socially, someone who isn't interested in the subject matter, someone who can't sit still or who is disruptive, someone whose parents meddle or are annoying or disengaged, someone who has awkward social skills, someone who complains, someone who is hard to teach, someone who isn't likable, someone who is accident prone, etc. Then I ask my students if their P-12 students experience or 'feel' these realities in their schools. Without exception they admit that almost every student knows who the ideal student is (or what qualities make up such a person) and, thus, can measure their own status based on that exemplar. Ideal students most often know they are ideal because they are nearer to the narrative of the ideal student circulating in the culture of their school. And, non-ideal students feel the sting of comparison as they often fail to measure up to the meta-narrative that they swim in. Because the narrative of the 'ideal' has cache (or as Foucault writes, is value-laden) for both teachers and students alike, it becomes a motivating force. Student want to succeed, they want to be an ideal student. When they do, they bask in those accolades. And, when they don't, they feel 'dumb'they see themselves as 'bad at math' or a 'poor test-taker' or bad at school. That sense of comparison, then, pushes 'poor' students to work harder and 'get better' at school so that they too might feel the accolades of the ideal student.

"The important point here is that one finds one's place, one knows one's progress, through individuation—through the way that one stacks up against others making the same journey. In essence, dividing practices not only individuate the person by creating individuals separated from other individuals: but they also establish grids of individual ranking in order to motivate and evaluate individuals" (Jacobson 2010a, 266). Foucault contends that the norm that we hold out in our dividing practices,

> is established as a principle of coercion in teaching with the introduction of a standardized education and the establishment of the *ecoles normales* (teachers' training colleges); it is established in the effort to organize a national medical profession and a hospital system capable of operating general norms of health; it is established in the standardization of industrial processes and products. Like surveillance and with it, normalization becomes one of the great instruments of power at the end of the classical age. For the marks that once indicated status, privilege, and affiliation were increasingly replaced—or at least supplemented—by a whole range of degrees of normality indicating membership of a homogeneous social body, but also playing a part in classification, hierarchization, and the distribution of rank. In a sense, the power of normalization imposes homogeneity; but it individualizes by making it possible to measure gaps, to determine levels, to fix specialities, and to render the differences useful by fitting them on to another. It is easy to understand how the power of the norm functions within a system of formal equality, since within a homogeneity that is the rule, the norm introduces, as a useful imperative and as a result of measurement, all the shading of individual differences. (1995, 184)

According to Foucault, the ways students were trained in these "ecoles normales" (normal schools), was through creating grids of comparison and ranking, then distributing students across them. When a student knows the ideal, she is able to measure the distance between her effort, skill, etc. and that ideal. This, if the ideal is important within the system, motivates the student to shrink that gap. Measuring the "gaps" between students becomes foundational to motivating students to press forward, to move toward the norm. But, according to Foucault, these gaps mean something, and herein provides both their motivational and problematic nature. As Foucault argues, these gaps become "value-giving" (1995, 182) measurements. "Status becomes associated with normalization, and how one is progressing toward such a goal is *compared* to the gaps between oneself and another. 'Discipline rewards,' writes Foucault, 'simply by the play of awards, thus making it possible to attain higher ranks and places; it punishes by reversing this process' (1995, 181). Domination—the hierarchy of rising above another—becomes the means of status through individuation which in turn becomes both measurable and value-laden within regimes of disciplinary power and training and the dividing practices they employ" (Jacobson 2010a,267). But, what might this have to do with a bump game at Southside K-8?

Dividing Practices, Bullying and Schooling

Foucault might argue that the Southside incident wasn't an aberration, but instead was a product of the efficiency of schooling. The scenario worked because it made sense at Southside. Jake could have lain down on the bump court and cried in order to create status with his peers. Why didn't he? Because gaining status in that way would not have 'made sense' to the bump crowd. But, to gain status by publicly humiliating Matthew did. Why? Foucault would likely contend that "schooling and bullying are part of the same process of individuation—the creation of subjects measured by the gaps between them" (Jacobson 2010a, 268).[5] In other words, domination (being at the top of the pack) does equate with status, not necessarily as an innate aspect of human existence, but because the culture of motivation that we use to train students in schools dictates it. The worst student isn't honored; the best is. The weakest student isn't looked up to; the strongest and fastest is. The one being humiliated is not envied (i.e., Matthew); the one who dominates him is (i.e., Jake). "If we are to take Foucault seriously, school culture itself becomes complicit in the formation of the bully, the victim, and the space for bullying to become a viable option by which to secure privilege via an imbalance of power" (Jacobson 2010a, p. 268). Let's take this one step further to create a bit more clarity. How might status through dominance be connected to the gaps created by hierarchy within school discourse and practice? An extended quote from an earlier article will be helpful here:

"Schools today predominately motivate students through hierarchical individuation. For example, imagine a tenth-grade science teacher who announces on the first day of class that all students would automatically receive an "A" for a final grade. We imagine two responses in this scenario. First, motivation would likely decrease and students would not work as hard as they might in a graded system based on production assessment (i.e., they would let projects slide, not study as carefully for tests, etc.). Why? *Because it doesn't matter anyway. Studying won't get me a higher grade.* Second, we imagine that parents (and students), especially those of upper grade ranges, would be upset. Why? Because, grade differentiation reveals who works hard and who does not, who will make the cut and who will not, who will have the grades to get into Harvard and who will not. The assumption here is that differentiation is important both in school and in life. Hence, motivational discourse within schooling dictates that one finds one's place in comparison over and against one's classmates. Ranking becomes a means of motivation through differentiation" (Jacobson 2010a, 268).

I return, here, to my high school scenario. The notoriety of the 100 meant something because it contrasted with the lack of notoriety of the remaining 1100. The fact that the 1,100 were not 'special' and that they recognized the 'specialness' of the 100, made the status of the 100 meaningful. Consider, for example, the dreaded participation ribbon. When a student receives the participation ribbon (which everyone receives) it means far less to them than the first place ribbon (which only a few receive). When everyone is voted 'best personality' in high school, that designation becomes meaningless. It is only its exclusivity, in comparison with those who don't have the 'best personality' that gives it value. And that value is the very thing that motivates one to work harder to create a gap between them and their competition. This type of disciplinary training, creating student motivation, is deeply embedded in the fabric of schooling.

One might argue, here, that we should just move to non-graded schools. I have a friend who did just that with his high school band program. Feeling frustrated that his students were more highly motivated by the 'A' on their transcript than by a simply love of music, he tried an experiment; everyone automatically received an 'A' the first day of class. With the 'grading issue' out of the way, the band could simply focus on working hard and playing great music. What happened? Students didn't practice as much, because they weren't held accountable. The band progressively sounded worse throughout the year. After about a year grading was reintroduced and the band returned to its former glory. The truth is this type of individuated motivation (i.e., measuring gaps) works; that is why we continue to use it in schooling. But, what if we simply chose a different, less 'domineering' measure? For example, what if we measured students based on the relationships they developed with peers or on their involvement in service learning instead of how they stack up regarding grades or academic achievement? These types of measures seem much more altruistic. Quite quickly we imagine the same system coming into play. Though we've changed the measure (service instead of grades), students would likely begin to compete with each other regarding who has the most service learning hours or who has developed the best relational connections. Grades, or service learning hours, or 'niceness' aren't at issue here. No matter the measure, the system of hierarchical individuation that is foundational to modern schooling will continue to operate. It is the current narrative and all know it well. "Imagining schooling without such systems of ranking becomes almost impossible because . . . comparison and ranking have become so ingrained. In fact, such discourses become so prevalent that we can no longer imagine alternatives. They become normal.[6]

It is not difficult to imagine that within such systems where students find status over and against other students a normation of the ways status is established in general terms; that is, status through dominance. For example, standardization of all students aimed toward a single outcome, examinations to measure progress, motivation based upon grade comparison or work comparison (better students are honored), grade listings for all to see (names are removed, but one knows how one stacks up compared to the class mean), honor roles (often printed in school newspapers), etc. are a normal part of schooling. These practices continue to be points of comparison and motivation within schooling. More than a genetic delinquent, the bully follows closely the pathways provided by the dividing practices of discipline employed by schooling. The bully learns that it is through dominance (ranking higher) that valued status is achieved. The motivational discourse of schooling involves the notion that if one works hard one will get rewarded, and that reward is significant because of its differentiation (one becomes the star player, the star of the class play, the valedictorian, or a Harvard student while *others do not*). Some simply become worth more. While an in-depth Foucauldian analysis of school motivational discourse is beyond the scope of this chapter,[7] this brief example points to the ways that school discourse often mirrors the *gaining-of-status-over-and-against-a-weaker-student* that bullying exemplifies. We imagine the bully's search for subjectivity (who really counts and who does not) being impacted by such discourses. If the bully can rise above the victim, then hierarchical status is established and subjectivity is solidified (Jacobson 2007a)" (Jacobson 2010a, 268–269).

BULLYING AND REHABILITATION

Research indicates that, at least at some level, bullies need to be 'rehabilitated' through training and surveillance. To an extent, a bully is seen as someone who resists the anti-bullying rhetoric of schooling; who, perhaps because of poor family dynamics (e.g., dominating or distant parenting styles) or poor teacher modeling, has come to find satisfaction in the tears of a classmate. But, in this chapter I have sought to consider the forces have shaped Jake and, thus, where we might direct our primary interventions. If Jake is an outlier, a bad egg, then in our rehabilitative work he becomes the main site of intervention (i.e., we help him to be less angry, we train him to care more for Matthew, etc.). But, what do we do if we conclude that Jake has simply taken seriously the rhetoric of schooling? That he has come to believe the story that the dividing practices of schooling use to motive students to achieve: i.e., the one who dominates is the one who is valued?

> Foucault has helped us consider the possibility that Jake, instead, may be evidence that schooling itself is working. Of course, these are unintended consequences. Nonetheless, Jake simply mirrors more deeply the motivational discourses and practices of Southside. Certainly, there was a public non-bullying stance at Southside. But it seemed to have little effect on Jake. Jake, including his bullying, can be seen as a product not only of family, but of Southside itself. (Jacobson 2010a, 273)

Foucault describes the dividing practices that are employed in various settings, including schools; narratives that create grids of value that motivate toward the ideal. It could be argued that Jake, perhaps coming to Southside with bullying capacities instilled by family or other life situations, simply took seriously the 'status-by-comparison' rhetoric of schooling. On Foucault's view, Jake's desire to establish a valued place for the self to stand (status) is of the same cloth as status offered by the motivational discourses of schooling. Jake, it could be argued, is guilty of taking that narrative to its logical extreme. He who dominates secures valued status within school.[8]

CONCLUSION

In essence, I have sought to do two things in this chapter. First, and perhaps foremost, I have endeavored to elucidate the links between motivational discourse within schools and the form of 'status-acquisition-through-dominance' that bullying represents. Remember, if bullying is situated in a quest for status with peers (which I argued toward in Chapter 4), then what I have highlighted here is the pathway that such status-acquisition activities might take within schools. The culture of 'value-based-on-comparative-rank' is of the same cloth in both projects; schooling and bullying.

Second, in this chapter I have sought to consider in an indirect way the processes of training itself. Remember, Foucault's anthropology makes clear that the prison system moved from a focus on public punishment to undergird the position of the Sovereign to a rehabilitative project. Disciplinary training, along with its dividing practices, was aimed at rehabilitating the prisoner; reforming a bad egg. Here, the means of moral education (or, one might say, transformation) is exacted through punishment, dividing practices (training hands and creating grids of value), and surveillance. This mirrors many anti-bullying programs (awareness of bullying activities, stern talks with and reprimand of the bully, specific training to help them be less angry or have greater empathy, and surveillance to hold them accountable). In a sense, these are the components of our 'moral' education. But, according to Foucault, this rehabilitative project employed by prisons was and continues to be ineffective. Hence, we now come more squarely to the moral education foundational to our anti-bullying efforts. The real question becomes if the "I like" of Jake was bent on the public humiliation of Matthew, how might one go about changing that "I like"? In other words, how do we begin the work of helping a bully to no longer desire to bully? That is the project we take up in our next chapter.

6 Need, Stories, and Moral Life
Behavior Comes from Somewhere

In my undergraduate Foundations of Education course I pose a couple of questions to my students early in the semester. First, I ask them why on the first day of the class they didn't walk in and all gather behind the teaching podium. Or, why they didn't come in and organize themselves, lying perpendicular on the floor against the back wall. Instead, like 'good' students, they file in and, without any prompting, they sit behind the tables in the main section of the room. When I ask them why they did that, they simply reply: "that's how it works." In other words, the story of schooling involves students sitting in desks or behind tables, with a teacher typically up front teaching (or at least leading). Now granted, there are different teaching scenarios (outdoor school, student-led courses, etc.), but the fact that, without exception, each student walked in and found a chair behind a table tells us that the 'story' of schooling has been well communicated.

I then ask another question: "What if I were to tell you that to be someone important here on campus you'd need to climb to the top of the School of Education building and jump off the roof? Would you do it?" Their response? "Not on your life?" Why? "Because, that doesn't make any sense here. Tell me I need to get good grades or be on the soccer team and I might by in. But, who jumps off a roof to be someone on campus?" I push a bit further at this point. "What if I told you that to be someone of status on campus you'd need to slit your bottom lip, insert a plate, then sew it back up? The bigger the plate, the more status you'd have." Their response? "You're crazy!" They are correct; to ask them to do such a thing on campus, or even in America is ludicrous, if not sadistic. "But," I add, "if you were a part of a certain tribe in Africa, slitting your lip and inserting a plate would not only make sense, it would be the pathway to becoming a model and well-respected citizen of the tribe." What's the difference? The narratives that we believe direct not only our thinking (about who has status and who doesn't), but our behavior as well. I closed Chapter 5 by briefly discussing the story of 'dividing practices' that we employ within schooling to motivate students. In this chapter I shift the discussion to need, the stories that provide pathways of meeting need, and the ways moral education becomes transformative. Essentially, we will begin to think about the process of changing the heart, or disposition, of a bully (which, in my opinion, is the only real game in town!).

Christian Smith, in his book *Moral, Believing Animals: Human Personhood and Culture* (2003) raises an interesting perspective at the outset. "Many years ago," Smith explains,

> our human ancestors huddled around fires listening to shamans and elders telling imaginative stories by which they made sense of their world and their lives in it. They told myths about the world's origins, and about how they as people came to be. They told legends about mighty heroes of old, about overcoming great adversity, about visions of the future. They narrated tales of moral struggle, about people good and bad, and about what happens to naughty children. They recounted myths about fairies, spirits, gods, and powerful cosmic forces. By narrating such fictional stories, our ancestors recounted meaningful explanations of a world that was to them mysterious and dangerous—and entertained themselves in the process. As primitives, telling such stories, myths, and legends was the only way they knew how to explain the world and contemplate how to live in it. And such was the condition of traditional human societies of all kinds up until a few hundred years ago. (2003, 63)

"But all that has changed," Smith continues. "We moderns,"

> no longer have to huddle around fires telling fanciful myths about creations, floods, trials, conquests, and hoped-for paradises. Science, industry, rationality, and technology have dispelled the darkness and ignorance that once held the human race captive to its fanciful fables. Today, through progress, enlightenment, and cultural evolution, we now possess positive knowledge, scientific facts, rational analyses. We no longer need to be a people of ballads and legends, for we are a people of periodic tables, technical manuals, genetic maps, and computer codes. We may tell fables to our children about wolves and witches and arks. But the adult world is one of modern, scientific information, facts, and knowledge. We have left behind myths and legends. We are now educated, rational, analytical. Indeed, by struggling to break out of the fear and ignorance of our ancestral myth-making past into the clear daylight of rational, scientific knowledge, we have opened up for the human race a future of greater prosperity, longevity, and happiness. Such is the story we moderns—huddled around our televisions and computer work stations—like to tell each other. This is the dominant narrative by which we make sense of our world and the purpose of our lives in it. (2003, 63–64)

Smith makes a point to note that it's not that either, or any, of our stories are false.

Narratives, myths, and fables can be true, in their way. The point, rather, is that for all of our science, rationality, and technology, we moderns are no less the makers, tellers, and believers of narrative construals of existence, history, and purpose than were our forebears at any other time in human history. But more than that, we not only continue to be animals who make stories but also animals who are made by our stories. We tell and retell narratives that themselves come fundamentally to constitute and direct our lives. We, every bit as much as the most primitive or traditional of our ancestors, are animals who most fundamentally understand what reality is, who we are, and how we ought to live by locating ourselves within the larger narratives and metanarratives that we hear and tell, and that constitute what is for us real and significant. (2003, 64).

The stories of culture, Smith argues, that humans live within come to shape not only how we interpret reality, but the behaviors set within those realities. Hence, in a certain tribe in Africa we would gladly slit our lips to garner status within the village, while at the same time my Foundations of Education students are repulsed by such a practice. But, such stories do affect why my students might use public dominance to establish status with their peers, while in another culture such practices would be beyond comprehension. There are an almost unlimited trove of stories that might guide the ways we think about ourselves and the ways we might live. For example, the American dream is something that we continue to hold dearly here in the states. Thus, many see home ownership, retirement planning, raising children, and being better off than their parents as inherently important motivating factors in life. Different stories drive gang life in American cities; stories that guide who these young adolescent gang members talk to, where they hang out within the city, how status is achieved, what membership means, etc. The palette of stories is endless: religious, political, and social stories play out in our lives in far-reaching, yet fundamentally meaningful ways.

Certainly this concept is not new. Cultural anthropologists have advocated this reality for decades. My point here, bringing it back to my opening paragraph of the chapter, is that there is also a story of schooling; one which we constitute (i.e., put into place and further) and one which constitutes us (i.e., guides how we think about ourselves and others, as well as our behavior). In Chapter 5 I raised the notion of the ideal student, indicating that most of my students could articulate who that might be (e.g., someone who works hard, is interested and engaged, does well, progresses, gets along with others, who listens and follows directions, who dresses appropriately, etc.). In contrast, there is a corresponding story of the 'non-ideal' student, which often we equate as the antithesis of the ideal (e.g., someone who doesn't work hard, is disinterested, struggles, doesn't progress as expected, etc.). Of course, some of these attributes are possible avenues for a wide variety of students to take up (e.g., someone who works hard), but some literally lie outside of the control of any given student (e.g., parents who are engaged at the right level). My point here is not to parse which stories are good or bad, but instead to highlight the fact that these stories not only exist, but impact those within their purview. Certain students feel successful (the closer to the 'ideal' student one is, the more successful one feels—this mirrors our Foucault discussion in Chapter 5), while others feel dumb or like they don't fit. Certain teachers are excellent (depending on how close their students line up with the ideal), and others need remediation plans because their students are progressing toward the ideal. Here I to note that such stories matter in both an affective manner (i.e., how we feel) as well as in our practice (i.e., behaviors which we take up). As cultural anthropologists (such as Smith) argue, the stories we believe provide pathways of behavior.

So, why do stories matter, especially so when we consider the topic at the heart of moral education? Moral education certainly involves aspects of rule-making, policies, procedures, rewards, consequences and surveillance. Make it clear, then enforce the rules. This is a very similar model in place to foster traffic law compliance—where increasingly traffic cameras provide more detailed surveillance! Perhaps, then, we should simply employ more cameras around our school campuses to 'catch' bullies and, thus, curtail bullying activity. But, I question whether this will bring the imagined good result when it comes to complex human interactions such a bullying. Recalling to Kester and Mann's (2008) report focused on anti-bullying efforts in the state of Washington, two findings are salient to this notion:

> FINDING 5: Districts appear to have responded to their statutory requirement to have anti-bullying policies.
>
> FINDING 6: Bullying has not declined significantly in Washington public schools since 2002, based on statewide data. Slight changes have occurred in which kind of bullying is most common among grades, but the overall rates are stubbornly similar across years (2008, p. i).

Here, state law prohibiting harassment and bullying has been enacted, policies regarding bullying have been developed by all Washington state school districts, and procedures have been distributed (including training, reporting, and response guidelines) and yet, "bullying has not declined significantly" with only "slight changes" in the "kinds of bullying" across grade levels occurring. This begs the question, "what is moral education (if not simply establishing and communicating the 'rules,' then watching to make sure they are followed) and how might it be more effectively enacted?" I turn now to a brief discussion of moral education, seeking to shift our understanding of morality; moving from the notion of adherence to a set of rules via self-discipline to something much more deeply engrained in identity.

MORAL IDENTITY

Often, when it comes to moral education we move to the arguably religious notion of temptation. In other words, situations or opportunities arise which tempt us to 'do the wrong thing.' Through self-discipline or will power the morally upstanding individual resists that temptation and 'does what is right.' Here I don't intend to critique such a view, but instead to consider the role of *will* power in moral action. Will power, in fact, may be important to regulating moral life, but it is secondary to disposition. Will power first needs a *will*. Augusto Blasi in a chapter entitled "Moral Character: A Psychological Approach" argues that "to be able to consistently guide one's life according to moral aims, one needs the set of capacities that constitute willpower; most important one needs to put these capacities at the service of stable moral concerns" (2005, 78). Blasi contends that will power is one of many different tools that we can employ toward a number of ends. For example, will power is needed when I'm exhausted, but a neighbor needs help. Pushing past my tiredness, I will myself out off of my sofa and out to my neighbor's project. But, will power can also be used for different ends. A criminal would also need will power to overcome the fear involved in holding up a bank. Blasi argues that "one needs a different kind of will to set willpower in operation and provide it with a specific meaning; what one needs, with regard to moral character, is a will that desires and tends toward the moral good" (2005, 78). For example, in bullying if the will (or desire) of the bully is to stop bullying, then she may need more will power to stand up to her peers who may be encouraging her to continue targeting the victim. But, if his will or desire is to continue to bully, then the problem is not teaching him to 'resist' that which he believes it wrong, but to 'convince' him it's wrong in the first place. If the bully is bent on bullying, then our reprimand and surveillance, may just drive the bullying underground, when our real aim is to transform desire. "Hence, the direction that willpower is aimed (via desire) becomes crucial to moral character" (Jacobson 2009b, p. 68).

Higgins-D'Alessandro and Powers contend that the will, which for them directs moral judgment, is deeply tied to our sense of identity. "Moral judgments," the argue,

> thus appear to go further than rational assessments of the right and wrong of particular actions. Moral judgments seem to extend not simply to actions but to the agent. Individuals desire to be persons who act morally. In this sense, moral judgments involve the self. Failing to act morally may diminish one's sense of self and of self-worth, while acting morally may increase or at least maintain one's sense of self and of self-worth. . . . The starting point for our approach of character is the self as a responsible moral agent. Responsibility, as we noted above, ties moral judgment to moral action through the moral self. One of us (Higgins-D'Alessandro 2002) has been exploring responsibility

through open-ended interviews about everyday moral living. One of the simplest yet most startling outcomes of this study to date is that the problems that most individuals describe as moral are not whether a particular action is right or wrong but how to act responsibly in a situation with significant consequences for the self and often for others. (2005, 112–113)

Concurring, Blasi also ties morality to an inner unity of personhood:

> There is one kind of identity . . . that is intrinsically related to the highest integrity. This occurs when a person so identifies with his or her commitments, cherished values and ideals, that he or she constructs around them the sense of a central essential self. This sort of appropriation determines what "really matters" to the person; it establishes such a hierarchy among the person's goals and concerns as to create a sense of subjective unity and lifelong direction, and provides one with a sense of depth and necessity in his being.(2005, 92)

"Blasi is not arguing, here, toward a notion of an essential self that we are to search for and uncover, but instead for a sense of self that is constructed by individuals regarding who they want to be and what really matters to them. In essence, here, identity becomes based on the ideal self that one desires for oneself, thus affecting the *direction* one gives to one's will power" (Jacobson 2009b, 68).

Not long ago I had a conversation with one of our MEd students. We were considering the topic of moral education and I asked her to create a list of things she considered right (i.e., what she tries to be/do in life) and what she considered wrong (i.e., things she would never do). Fairly early in the conversation she clearly articulated her abhorrence of littering. We pushed further to understand her moral stand on littering. "How did that conviction get 'in you'?" I questioned. She wasn't exactly sure, other than she did acknowledge that her mother was adamantly opposed to littering as well. I then asked: "How hard would it be for you, seeing no garbage can in sight, to throw a gum wrapper on the path?" Without thought, and with great passion, she exclaimed, "never!" She would never deliberately litter if it was in her control not to. Of course people can be forced to do many things, but on her own this MEd student would do next to anything not to litter; she was *not* a litterbug! "Compromising one's identity," writes Blasi, "is felt to be unthinkable: it would be experienced as the most serious self-betrayal and as the total loss of one's self or soul" (2005, 92). In other words, when we come to see ourselves as a certain kind of person (identity) who, thus, acts in certain ways (behaviors), then our desires (will) work to direct our moral lives toward those aims. "I don't litter, because that's not who I am!" According to Higgins-D'Alessandro and Powers, character and identity are linked:

> When we speak of a person as having character, we typically mean that one can count on that person, even in very difficult circumstances. In the context of sports, individuals and teams typically display character by not folding under the most intense pressure. The etymological definition of character as a permanent mark or stamp seems to express this sense of steadfastness and dependability. Yet Walker (1998) points out that reliability should not be equated with immovability or rigidity. The reliable person is a responsive person. The reliable person adapts to new challenges and addresses past wrongs and wounds. (2005, 113)

"This directional self-identity becomes foundational to moral life" (Jacobson 2009b, 69).

A bully bullies for any number of reasons. Our intention is to help the bully to stop. We often do so by articulating clear rules, educating students and teachers, keeping a better eye on students (especially in unstructured areas), and meeting out rewards and punishments. And, for some bullies this seems to work; but, for research tells us that the effectiveness of such approaches are uneven at best or ineffective at worst. If, as Blaisi argues, willpower must be driven by 'will' itself, then changing that will or desire become paramount. What if a student, like my MEd student, was as adamantly opposed to dominating and humiliating a classmate as she was to littering? If we can change will, I argue, then we create a fighting chance to change behavior. If we don't, then we simply set up the scenario for a more covert, better-trained bully. But if moral behavior is linked to moral identity, then how is such identity formulated? To address this difficult question I turn to the work of John Dewey and his influential work *Democracy and Education*.

DEWEY AND MORAL EDUCATION

In his *Pedagogical Creed* John Dewey argues that,

> Moral education centers upon this conception of the school as a mode of social life, that the best and deepest moral training is precisely that which one gets through having to enter into proper relations with others in a unity of work and thought. The present educational systems, so far as they destroy or neglect this unity, render it difficult or impossible to get any genuine, regular moral training. (2000, 95)

Dewey argues that moral education, and he would contend any kind of education, is always a social endeavor. In fact, the most effective 'moral training' comes not through the 'dividing practices' outlined by Foucault, but through students entering into 'proper relations' with each other. Dewey is adamant that if we neglect these 'proper relations' which allow for the 'unity of work and thought' we will find great difficulty in exacting any real, moral education. But, what does Dewey mean by 'moral education' and what kinds of social interaction would equate to 'proper relations'?

In *Democracy and Education* Dewey asserts that, "The development within the young of the attitudes and dispositions necessary to the continuous and progressive life of a society cannot take place by direct conveyance of beliefs, emotions, and knowledge" (1944, 22). It seems, at least in part, that what Dewey means by moral life is a life that stems from our social attitudes and dispositions. "For example, we might call a man "moral" who is careful to never break the speed limit (maintaining a disposition to live lawfully). We might call a young woman "moral" who chooses not to steal from her employer (maintaining an attitude that such behavior is contrary to the employer-employee relationship). A young middle-schooler may choose not to bully a classmate, perhaps even coming to the victim's aid, because he believes (attitudes) that such actions are "wrong" and is compelled (disposition) to take action. Might we not also call such a stand moral? In short, attitudes and dispositions shape our interactions. More pointedly, Dewey clarifies the link between such disposition and democratic behavior. Dewey argues that the 'social environment forms the mental and emotional disposition of behavior in individuals by engaging them in activities that arouse and strengthen certain impulses, that have certain purposes and entail certain consequences' (1944, 16). Dewey, then, links such dispositions specifically to moral development and schooling. 'Schools remain,' Dewey contends, '. . . the typical instance of environments framed with express reference to influencing the mental and moral disposition of their members' (1944, 19)" (Jacobson 2010c, 47).

"But, how are such moral dispositions formed? Dewey argues that they are engendered socially. Dewey asserts that the inculcation of "beliefs, emotions, and knowledge" linked to attitudes and dispositions does not take place via *direct conveyance*, but instead is a product of one's environment. The Southside administration attempted to convey "beliefs" (bullying is wrong), "emotions" (stern reprimands aimed at creating a fear of reprisal), and "knowledge" (the fact that the bullying was hurtful to Matthew and was a violation of school rules) directly. The bullies were then watched to ensure compliance, but to no avail. Dewey contends that when one is "trained" by the use of direct pressure (e.g., reward, punishment, surveillance) aimed at commanding conformity, often one's "instincts remain attached to their original objects of pain or pleasure (1944, 13)" (Jacobson 2010c, 47). In other words, the behavior is linked to the pleasure or pain brought to bear by outside forces (a teacher, a parent), but not to a fundamental change in disposition or attitude. Hence, when under the watchful eye of an adult the student may feign conformity, only to transgress such rules once outside of the purview of supervision.

Dewey contrasts such training with the conception of inward dispositional transformation as a result of *common participation*. "When one," Dewey contends, really shares or participates in the common activity . . . his original impulse is modified. He not merely acts in a way agreeing with the actions of others, but, in so acting, the same ideas and emotions are aroused in him that animate the others. . . . [The social environment] forms the mental and emotional disposition of behavior in individuals by engaging them in activities that arouse and strengthen certain impulses, that have certain purposes and entail certain consequences. (1944, 13, 14, 16)

This becomes reminiscent of Blasi's notion of identity which gives direction to one's will power. In other words, like Blasi, Dewey would argue that when "moral" education is primarily based upon the communication of rules, then surveillance meant to enforce such rules it becomes ineffective precisely because it often fails to affect the heart. Disposition is not so much a matter of conformity to someone else's rules, but staying true to our own rules; those rules that have become a part of our identity (and, thus, affecting the *direction* one gives to one's willpower). On this plane, Blasi and Dewey's philosophy of moral education find resonance with each other. Further, according to Dewey, identity is most deeply constructed socially. And, it is this social participation, the back and forth movement reminiscent of democracy, that Dewey believes is, in and of itself, moral. Remember, Dewey argues that the "best and deepest moral training is precisely that which one gets through having to enter into proper relations with others in a unity of work and thought" (2000, 95).

Dewey claims that through common participation individuals can be brought into "like-mindedness" (i.e., of a similar fabric or identity) within a community and that, in this participation, attitudes and dispositions are formed and re-formed. Of course the fact that individuals are "environed" by the cultures within which they live is a fairly common-sensical notion. Dewey, though, would contend that this social environing must be due to more than simple habit (mindless mimicry), but is fostered through communication which informs and connects individual thinking (including attitudes and dispositions) and action with others in the community. Hence, rather than educating directly, Dewey asserts that the role of a teacher is to create environments which connect with *individual student capacities*. Capacity, for Dewey, does not denote a void to be filled, but a potential that may be tapped. Each student comes with certain histories, certain interests that educative efforts must engage toward the ends of further growth. Outlining this "differentiated interest" Dewey argues that "one who recognizes the importance of interest will not assume that all minds work in the same way because they happen to have the same teacher and textbook. Attitudes and methods of approach and response vary with the specific appeal the same material makes, this appeal itself varying with *difference of natural aptitude, of past experience, of plan of life, and so on*" (1944, 130 emphasis mine) (Jacobson 2009b, 71).

In one sense we imagine Dewey arguing that moral education is focused on providing 'proper social experiences' that will instill "specific common attitudes and dispositions that are "right" or that further democratic or societal life" (Jacobson 2010c, 48). While Dewey would likely agree that establishing proper social interactions is foundational to moral development (in fact, he would argue that without an emphasis on these interactions it becomes nearly impossible to provide 'any genuine, regular moral training'!), he would bristle at the notion of establishing a list or rights and wrongs, especially in public, pluralistic settings. In fact, this has been one of the more difficult aspects of thinking about moral education within schools. We always ask, "who's morals?"[1] But, Dewey's understanding of moral education goes deeper than a list of virtues. Dewey extrapolates his view of the morals we educate toward in the last chapter of *Democracy and Education*, bringing us full circle regarding the interaction between social and moral life. "All of the separations," Dewey summarizes,

> which we have been criticizing [throughout *Democracy and Education*]—and which the idea of education set forth in the previous chapters is designed to avoid—spring from taking morals too narrowly,—giving them, on one side, a sentimental goody-goody turn without reference to effective ability to do what is socially needed, and, on the other side, overemphasizing convention and tradition so as to limit morals to a list of definitely stated acts. As a matter of fact, *morals are as broad as acts which concern our relationships with each other.* (1944, 357)

Morals, for Dewey, are integral to our relationships with each other. For Dewey, more than a list of "rights" and "wrongs," morals are be equated with democratic life and all that it entails. Dewey continues: "morals concern nothing less than the whole character and the whole character is identical with the man in all his concrete make-up and manifestations" (1944, 357–358). Like Blasi, Dewey believes that morals come out of identity; identity that is established within the milieu of social interaction. Dewey contends that "to possess virtue does not signify to have cultivated a few nameable and exclusive traits; it means to be fully and adequately what one is capable of becoming *through association with others* in all the offices of life" (1944, 358, emphasis mine). "We are morally made, or formed, in our associations with others. And, hence, we—morally—reflect the very nature of those associations. And, here, we come to the point, as Dewey eloquently and powerfully summarizes in *Democracy and Education*: "The moral and the social quality of conduct are, in the last analysis, identical with each other" (1944, 358). One, then, might argue that the "proper relations" of the classroom are in and of themselves moral, and that helping students to grow in and attend to such proper relations is at the heart of their own moral formation. For, as students live in such mutuality their character begins to reflect that moral interaction—they are trained, not via direct conveyance, but through the medium of the environment. In essence, their character begins to reflect that environment; they reflect the "properly social" effected in relationship with each other" (Jacobson 2010c, 49).

NEED, CULTURE, AND MORAL EDUCATION

In Chapter 4 I argued that a primary need that drives much bullying activity is the need to create status with peers. In Chapter 5 I argued that one pathway to gain status in the story of schooling is through domination. How we 'stack up' in comparison with our classmates determines our standing in the eyes of all who watch in schooling. And, as the story of schooling goes, the one on top is the one who is valued. In this chapter, I have argued three things: first, stories (cultures) direct the ways that we meet need; two, moral life is situated in disposition as opposed to following someone else's rules (i.e., we live out of who we believe ourselves to be, rather than who someone else requires us to be); third, in somewhat circular fashion, moral identity is established socially (in the face-to-face interactions of social and cultural interaction). Hence, we do things for reasons. Bullying is an expression of some need. If that need is centered in creating identity with our peers, students then look for available pathways within the narrative of schooling to meet that need (being the star quarterback, being the best writer, etc.). Domination (being on top) often makes sense as a pathway to status within schools. Very few students try to get the worst score on a test or seek to be the worst player on the team, hoping to get cut! The question, then, becomes how do we help a bully no longer want to publicly dominate a classmate? How do we change disposition? For Dewey, that kind of moral education happens only through the social environments we find ourselves within. Students are trained morally not through rules or direct conveyance, but through the kinds of cultures that environ them. This, in my opinion, begins to offer up fertile ground in understanding the kinds of moral transformation that may move a bully to no longer *desire* to bully. Before laying out more of a blueprint for this process in schools, I want to delve into this notion a bit more deeply. In Chapter 7 I will consider Imre Lakatos' work focused on the kinds of things that keep us from making a shift in worldview (why we resist moving from one belief—e.g., littering is just fine—to an alternative belief—e.g., I would never litter!). Next, in Chapter 7 I will consider an unlikely source, Bloom's Taxonomy not as directed toward 'knowledge,' but toward affective transformation. And, finally, in Chapter 7, I will put some feet to this discussion by considering Vivian Paley's work in a kindergarten classroom where she seeks to institute a new rule, a new way of being, among her students; seeking to alter the already-embedded social practice of choosing friends and rejecting undesirables.

7 Re-Storying a School
Resistance, Taxonomy, and Kindergarten

To this point I have raised the notion at several points that if we are to effectively address bullying in schools we must affect desire. Our surveillance can seldom be complete enough (e.g., consider the increasing threat and activity involved in cyber bullying which most often takes place from the students own home) to catch every nuance of bullying through the school day, let alone on the weekends! In fact, Rachel Simmons reminds us that even when we are directly watching students interact, we may not see the bullying that is transpiring right in front of us.[1] More to the point, in this project I am fundamentally interested in stopping bullying before it happens. And here, I have argued that unless we affect the desire to bully in the first place we will struggle as parents, teachers, and administrators. Dewey contends that in order to change disposition (which I am operationalizing to some degree as 'desire') we must pay attention to and literally create educational experiences/cultures which allow for like-mindedness in very specific ways. I have also argued that, on a Foucaldian view, the rhetoric of schooling may actually encourage the notion of gaining status through dominance (which I have argued is a salient component of bullying activity). Yet, here we're confronted with a need for greater clarity.

As I have intimated, most states now have on the books laws against harassment, intimidation, and bullying. In fact, most school districts are now required to adopt specific policies, procedures and training (of both students and teachers) aimed toward reducing bullying activities. One could argue that even though we still operate schooling on a comparative hierarchical value system (which I find deeply problematic in our anti-bullying efforts), still schools are actively working to change mindsets through education, training, and response. Why, then, aren't we seeing a general drop in school bullying incidents? I will touch on two important reasons in this chapter and the next. First, I believe that we will only see a change in bullying activity when we change the story of schooling; i.e., we must re-story school culture, considering motivation and value within the story of schooling. I will pursue this more fully in Chapter 8. Second, we need to understand the processes of becoming 'like-minded' and the resistance that is inherent in such transformation. To better understand this latter issue

I will consider three pictures of transformation, beginning with the work of Imre Lakatos as he seeks to understand the processes and resistance to theoretical shifts within the scientific community.

LAKATOS, THE HARD CORE, AND PROTECTIVE BELTS

We often carry with us a rationalistic approach to mental shifts. This is certainly true when it comes to moral education (we teach students about bullying, working to *convince* them that it is inappropriate and that it is an activity in which they should not engage). If we can build a case (so the moral rhetoric goes), then we can produce a rational shift (oh my gosh, I didn't know that our activity in the bump game was so painful to Matthew; or, I didn't know that what we were doing in the bump game was actually bullying), thus changing behavior. I am not discounting that our minds must be involved in such shifts, but Imre Lakatos complicates such a picture of transformation.

Change within the scientific community (i.e., scientists moving from one theory to another) is often viewed as linear, crucial experiment (a definitive new study that proves something is true) dependent, and instantaneous. Lakatos in his classic essay *Falsification and the Methodology of Scientific Research Programmes* (1970) compares this view of rational transformation with a careful history of how theories within the scientific community actually evolve and shift. Interestingly, Lakatos asks whether science is based on rationality or religion (i.e., belief). Lakatos' research refutes the idea that scientists simply shift to a new worldview or theory when another, more convincing (or provable) explanation arises. "How are research programmes eliminated?" asks Lakatos. "Our scientific folklore . . . is impregnated with theories of instant rationality" (1970, 172). Here, most of us operate on the view that once we see or hear contrary evidence, human beings (including scientists who are seen to be objective and crucial-experiment driven), simply shift to a new view. "But," continues Lakatos, "the novelty of a factual proposition can frequently be seen only after a long period has elapsed" (1970, 155). Lakatos concludes by roundly claiming that "there are no such things as crucial experiments" (1970, 173).

In contrast to Lakatos' findings, we often hold to the more simplistic view in any kind of change; i.e., if you offer convincing proof, I will simply change my mind. For example, one may believe that the sun revolves around the earth. But, through a new experiment, proof is offered that strongly points to the fact that the earth actually revolves around the sun. After this proving or decisive evidence is revealed, so the story goes, we change our mind and see the world differently (Jacobson 2007a).

The view here is that we are rational beings, and if we can be convinced rationally that our thinking/viewpoints are faulty we will quickly change those positions. Instead, Lakatos argues that we (including scientists) are beings that 'believe' and those beliefs are situated in what he calls hardcore beliefs, protected by auxiliary theories (or secondary beliefs). Hard core theories are the foundational belief (e.g., I believe the sun revolves around the earth), while auxiliary theories form a vast web of understanding which support and protect the hard core (e.g., the way the sun seems to move across the sky, the 'fact' that the earth feels stationary, the idea that humans are at the center of the universe, the seemingly biblical notion that the earth is central to 'creation,' etc.—this is what I believe!). These, contends Lakatos, are the auxiliary beliefs that prevented scientist from being open to Copernican theories (even though his evidence was strong) and that led them to brand him a heretic. "It is this protective belt," Lakatos argues,

> of auxiliary hypotheses which has to bear the brunt of tests and get adjusted and re-adjusted, or even completely replaced, to defend the thus-hardened core. [. . .] This 'core' is 'irrefutable' by the methodological decision of its protagonists: anomalies must lead to changes only in the 'protective' belt of auxiliary, 'observational' hypothesis and initial conditions. (1970, 133)

In Lakatos' view, a single theory is enmeshed within a web of ideas. It is protected, supported, and substantiated within those webs of understanding. These webs become tied to belief (science favoring corroborating experiments and resisting—often by explaining away through some auxiliary theory—experiments that threaten hard core theories). Theories become stubborn and the desire to maintain them (which, again, is situated in complex webs of understanding) resists change, thus making rational transformation arduous and uneven (Jacobson 2007a, 1939).

As Christian Smith argues, Lakatos too finds that humans are, indeed, moral believing animals, more than rational robots who take in new evidence and quickly adopt new theories based on that contrary evidence.[2] Lakatos' theory of rational transformation involves several important aspects. According to Lakatos, all theories are embedded in webs of understanding, making the process of transformation uneven, slow, even accidental.

> Rational transformation comes not from attacking one theory, but by breaking through a web of auxiliary theories that protect a hard core understanding. Because of these webs of meaning, change comes slowly and unevenly (non-instantaneously). Thus transformation involves an openness to consider alternative theories (while our tendency is to dismiss them out of hand), allowing them time to prove or disprove themselves. Transformation, then, comes in small steps, is often accidental, and often crucial points of change are only noticeable in hindsight. (Jacobson 2007a, 1939–1940)

If this is how transformation happens in the scientific community, what might this look like in our attempts to bring a moral/rational transformation in the mind/heart of a bully? What might we imagine to be the 'hard core' of bullying? For example, let's assume (as I have argued earlier) that at least to some degree bullying is a way to secure status in the eyes of my peers. What, then, might be the auxiliary beliefs that form a protective belt around this hard core? "When I publicly target Matthew in the bump game, my peers cheer and smile at me. This works!" "In school, the one who comes out on top is the one who's looked up to. Status is dependent upon hierarchy." "People agree with me when I bully." "A bully is a 'certain kind of person' and that person is strong. Survival of the fittest is a way of life." "Winning means others will lose. Dominance is power. Dominance is status and status is power." If, indeed, the bully believes these and other auxiliary beliefs, then when I attack the hard-core (i.e., you need to stop bullying), according to Lakatos we could expect to find little transformation. Telling someone to stop bullying, when that belief is embedded within a web of protective/supportive/auxiliary similar to those listed above, is like asking a hungry man not to eat the food in front of him.

If this is an accurate picture of theory transformation, then how do scientific shifts take place and, further, what advice would Lakatos give to scientists in order to help them to not allow 'religion' to discount new 'truths'? "Purely negative, destructive criticism," argues Lakatos

> like 'refutation' or demonstration of an inconsistency does not eliminate a programme. Criticism of a programme is a long and often frustrated process and one must treat budding programmes leniently (p. 179). But the psychology of science is not autonomous; for the—rationally reconstructed—growth of science takes place essentially in the world of ideas, in Plato's and Popper's 'third world', in the world of articulated knowledge which is independent of knowing subjects. (1970, 179, 80)

Here Lakatos contends that for scientists to accept, or buy into, a new theory (whether of the solar system or evolutionary processes) it will take more than new evidence and new claims. Dewey couches this notion in what he calls moral education through 'direct conveyance,' contending that some other kind of process is involved in lasting moral education. If the old 'core understandings' are, indeed, protected by an entire belt of protective ideas, then a number of responses become meaningful. First, we must realize that scientific theories stand in the 'world of ideas,' perhaps more helpfully, in the realm of belief. The process of change (as one moves from one 'religious belief' to another) is slow, is embedded in long conversations, and demands careful and repeated argument. Second, this transformational process also must focus initially not on the core belief, but on the auxiliary band that protects it. We must begin to help the audience rethink what a religious document might say about a solar-centric universe, or the perception that indeed the sun does seem to move across the sky, etc. *Beginning* with the 'sun as center' argument becomes futile as these auxiliary beliefs shield any progress toward transformation. Finally, Lakatos contends that those on the other side of the equation; i.e., those we are trying to convince, must maintain a level of patient openness. "All this suggests that we must not discard a budding research programme simply because it has so far failed to overtake a powerful rival. We should not abandon it if, supposing its rival were not there, it would constitute a progressive problemshift" (1970, 157). In other words, scientists should be trained to be tentative, to hold loosely the 'truths' they believe, understanding that the process of coming to new, more accurate understanding demands such openness. In many ways this seems contrary to the 'culture' of science (which is often based on proven theory predicated upon solid experimental evidence), and, in some ways, contrary to the culture of schooling (based on correct and repeatable knowledges) as well. Here, change does not come from one skirmish. In order to create change we must create a new world of ideas, slowly, methodically and over time and, at the same time, we must work to develop certain dispositions in our scientists (ones that are open as compared to solidly sure). Foundationally Lakatos challenges the pure rationality involved in change (transformation), even for scientists. He likens the positions we hold, which inform the behaviors we take up, much more akin to belief than to a more mechanistic evidence-based response. As outlined in the previous chapter, Dewey argues that any moral shift (and in fact any education at all) is enacted within cultures of openness. Moral life, more than being taught a list of polemics/truths that we follow, is something that is formed within us (i.e., we become like-minded) through the cultures within which we live. In some ways it seems less 'rational' and more cultural; less logical and more *affective*. But, what is the 'domain' that desire might be more situated in if it is not simply a rational process? I now move to discuss Bloom's Taxonomy, not of knowledge, but of affect.

BLOOM'S AFFECTIVE TAXONOMY

Benjamin S. Bloom out of the University of Chicago developed, in conjunction with others, a familiar and deeply used 'taxonomy' of knowledge. *The Taxonomy of Educational Objectives, Handbook I: Cognitive Domain* (1956), better known as 'Bloom's Taxonomy' has and continues to provide an outline of levels of deepening cognitive knowledge. Bloom's Taxonomy, or Bloom's classification system, has come to be synonymously associated with the cognitive processes of learning and using information or knowledges, moving in level of complexity from simple recall (memorization of facts) to comprehension, application, analysis, synthesis, and finally evaluation. According to this taxonomy, as students move from the lowest cognitive functions (memorizing) to the most complex (being able to evaluate based on facts, comprehension, synthesis, etc.), their level of cognitive fluency increases. In other words, stronger knowledge allows for not just 'regurgitation of details,' but the ability to apply knowledge in creative and meaningful ways.

For many teacher preparation programs, Bloom's Taxonomy continues to be a mainstay guide as teachers consider increasing the cognitive steps (i.e., leaning) of their students. But, per the title at the outset of this section, Bloom et al. had intended that the cognitive domain be the first objective in a three volume library. Bloom and his colleagues had originally set out to map not only the cognitive domain, but the affective and psychomotor domains as well. For he and his colleagues all three domains were instrumental to the educational process. Hence, in 1964 Krathwohl, Bloom and Masia penned their second volume in the set: *Taxonomy of Educational Objectives, Handbook II: Affective Domain*.

According to Krathwohl et al., the affective domain involves, "Objectives which emphasize a feeling tone, an emotion, or a degree of acceptance or rejection. Affective objectives vary from simple attention to selected phenomena to complex but internally consistent qualities of character and conscience. We found," they expound, "a large number of such objectives in the literature expressed as interests, attitudes, appreciations, values, and emotional sets or biases" (1964, 7). Immediately here, one will notice language akin to Dewey's 'attitudes' or 'dispositions' (values), ultimately important to any program of moral education (e.g., our anti-bullying work). Hence, understanding a taxonomy (perhaps even a progression) of values and attitudes holds promise in our endeavor to better understand the kinds of transformations necessary to curtail bullying activities.

Krathwohl et al. begin their volume on the affective domain by underscoring the fact that modern schooling has become much more focused on the cognitive domain (the informational, skill-based knowledges measured on standardized tests) to the exclusion of the affective domain centered in desire and attitudes. This does not mean that schooling does not care about such realities, and certainly the current movement to eradicate bullying within schools underlines the notion that schools are, indeed, still involved in such 'heart' educational processes. But, Krathwohl et al. argue that even when schools do take up 'moral' education it is often with the belief that such transformation is similar, if not identical, to cognitive growth. Discussing this shift (to cognitive education), Krathwohl et al. argue:

> Thus, the teacher's responsibility was reduce to that of providing learning experiences to develop the information in students, and the examination was designed to appraise the students' progress toward the information objectives. As a result of the research and writings of Tyler (1934; 1951), Furst (1958), Dressel (1958), and others this belief in the

'automatic' development of the higher mental processes is no longer widely held. However, there still persists an implicit belief that if cognitive objectives are developed, there will be a corresponding development of appropriate affective behaviors. Research summarized by Jacob (1957) raises serious questions about the tenability of this assumption. The evidence suggests that affective behaviors develop when appropriate learning experiences are provided for students much the same as cognitive behaviors develop from appropriate learning experiences. . . . Perhaps one of the most dramatic events highlighting the need for progress in the affective domain was the publication of Jacob's Changing Values in College (1957). He summarizes a great deal of educational research at the college level and finds almost no evidence that college experiences produce a significant change in students' values, beliefs, or personality. (1964, 19, 20)

In light of this belief that the processes for cognitive and affective growth are likely nuanced, nonetheless, there was a belief that like the cognitive domain, the affective domain would also be a structured set. Hence, Krathwohl and his colleagues began a "search for a continuum that would provide a means of ordering and relating the different kinds of affective behavior. It was presumed that the affective domain, like the cognitive, would be structured in a hierarchical order such that each category of behavior would assume achievement of the behaviors categories below it (1964, 24). While searching for a guiding taxonomy, or structure, of the affective domain, Krathwohl et al. also came to believe that progressing through such a structure would involve a process of 'internalization.' An extended quote focused on this process will be helpful here. "The more we carefully studied the components, however," contend Krathwohl et al.

The clearer it became that a continuum might be derived by appropriately ordering them. Thus the continuum progressed from a level at which the individual is merely aware of a phenomenon [e.g., know that bullying happens], being able to perceive it. At a next level he is willing to attend to phenomena [e.g., pay attention to the bullying around him or herself with some level of interest]. At a next level he responds to the phenomena with a positive feeling [e.g., or negative feeling when he or she sees bullying being played out against a classmate]. Eventually he may feel strongly enough to go out of his way to respond [e.g., to intervene in a bullying episode]. At some point in the process he conceptualizes his behavior and feelings and organizes these conceptualizations into a structure [e.g., I am on a mission to pay attention to and stop bullying]. This structure grows in complexity as it becomes his life outlook [e.g., this is who I am; not only will I never bullying another, but I'll work to stop it when I see it and before it happens]. (1964, 27)

Interestingly, this sounds very similar to Blasi's notion outlined in Chapter 6, likening character and value to an internalization process connected with identity. "This process or continuum," continues Krathwohl et al., "seemed best described by a term which was heard at various times in our discussions and which has been used similarly in the literature: 'internalization.' This word seemed an apt description of the process by which the phenomenon or value successively and pervasively become a part of the individual" (1964, 28). Thus, the affective taxonomy outlined by Krathwohl et al., founded in this notion of internalization, is "viewed as a process through which there is at first an incomplete and tentative adoption of only the overt manifestations of the desired behavior and later a more complete adoption" (1964, 29). Thus, Krathwohl et al. came to understand that as one moved more deeply through the affective domain (i.e., moving from an awareness of the rules to a 'desire' to follow the rules), it fundamentally involved a process of internalization; moving from outward pressure to inward disposition.

> Thus at the lowest end of the continuum, inner control serves only to direct attention. At higher levels, inner control produces appropriate responses, but only at the bidding of an external authority. At still higher levels, inner control produces the appropriate response even in the absence of an external authority. Indeed at still higher levels, these responses are produced consistently despite obstacles and barriers. (1964, 30)

Krathwohl et al. mapped five levels or classifications within the affective domain, beginning with the lowest or least internalized stage (receiving) and moving to the most integrated level (characterization). A brief description of each domain will be useful here.

1.0 Receiving (attending). Here the individual is aware of the phenomenon or rule or requirement. Here, the student is willing to receive direction or input, but their attention is controlled or selected by an outside force (e.g., a teacher who states and enforces the rule). It's interesting here that at its lowest level the affective domain requires openness. Many will likely argue simply getting to a point where a student is open to direction is often a significant task. We will come back to this, and to some degree have already opened this topic in Chapter 6, but suffice it note that this is Krathwohl's starting point.

2.0 Responding. Here the individual is open to response, willing to follow the rule or take up the value and may even find satisfaction in doing so.

3.0 Valuing. Here the student moves beyond simple behavior, to valuing the rule or phenomenon (remember, this not only applies to moral behavior—not being involved in bullying; but to other affective state—learning to love and appreciate literature). Here the individual values or perhaps prefers a certain disposition, even carrying a conviction or commitment toward it.

4.0 Organization. Here the student conceptualizes (build a framework, a world view) of the phenomenon or behavior, perhaps even building a case for it. The phenomenon or rule is organized into the individual's value system.

5.0 Characterization by a value or value complex. Here is the ultimate internalization; the rule, phenomenon or behavior becomes settled in the student's identity. "Oh, I wouldn't never to that. That's just not me!"

To flesh this out a bit more, Krathwohl et al. further delineate the five main components into subcomponents. Those include:

1.0 Receiving
- 1.1 Awareness—an awareness of the rule, issue, etc.
- 1.2 Willingness to Receive—a willingness or openness to the rule, issue, etc.
- 1.3 Controlled or Selected Attention—giving some attention to the rule, issue, etc., either under compulsion or on a voluntary basis.

2.0 Responding
- 2.1 Acquiescence in Responding—giving in to the rule, issue, etc.
- 2.2 Willingness to Respond—a willingness to respond or follow the rule, issue, etc.
- 2.3 Satisfaction in Response—actually feeling 'good' for following the rule, engaging the issue, etc.

3.0 Valuing
- 3.1 Acceptance of a Value—an inner confirmation that the rule, issue is of value.
- 3.2 Preference for a Value—a value preference (i.e., choosing it over other options) for the rule, issue, etc.
- 3.3 Commitment—a willed decision to follow the rule or engage the issue.

4.0 Organization
- 4.1 Conceptualization of a Value—beginning to build/adopt a framework around the rule, issue, etc.
- 4.2 Organization of a Value System—developing an organized and coherent framework around the rule, issue, etc. (i.e., a cogent argument, with supporting arguments, around the value of the rule, issue, etc.).

5.0 Characterization by a Value Complex
- 5.1 Generalized Set—the rule, issue, etc. is adopted as something "I" follow.
- 5.2 Characterization—the rule, issue, etc. is consistent with who I am; to live or act contrary to the rule is 'out of character' for me (Krathwohl et al. 1964, p. 37).

Re-Storying a School 93

Mapped across this taxonomy are five levels of internalization:
- Interest—I am interested in the rule, issue, etc.
- Appreciation—I appreciate, or see the value of the rule, issue, etc.
- Attitude—my attitudes are altered by the rule, issue, etc.
- Value—I deem the rule, issue, etc. as important.
- Adjustment—I make behavioral, willed decisions based on the rule, issue, etc. (Krathwohl 1964, 37).

The interesting thing for my purposes is where these 'affective' components engage the taxonomy. Here, if we want to move students from an awareness of bullying to an adjustment in not only how they think, but their behavior when it comes to bullying, this progression becomes significant. How, then, does Krathwohl et al. map internalization across the affective taxonomy?

In Figure 7.1, we see listed on the right what Krathwohl et al. call 'common affective terms.' These terms relay foundational elements of internalization when it comes to moral or inner transformation. We notice that interest begins with the foundational classification (1.0 Receiving; Awareness) and spans several domains, pushing partly through the 'valuing' level. Appreciation, which denotes more than simple awareness, moving more toward ownership begins a bit further in the process, yet culminates (or transitions) in about the same place as interest. A change in attitude, which Dewey sees as foundational to the type of moral education that we've been discussing, picks up from simple interest or even appreciation and leads the student into the initial work of organizing meaning regarding the phenomenon or behavior. Here students move past a simple awareness or interest in bullying, and begin to conceptualize a framework of understanding surrounding it. We see also that 'valuing' (deeming something important) and attitudes roughly occupy the same space. This makes sense, since to value something (e.g., that bullying is not an activity to be taken up) means that our attitudes toward it also shift (and vice versa). Finally, we notice what Krathwohl et al. call 'adjustment.' This, beginning in the 'response' phase, moves the candidate closer and closer to an ultimate internalization;

Interest	1.1 Awareness	→	3.2 Preference for a Value
Appreciation	1.3 Controlled or Selected Attention	→	3.2 Preference for a Value
Attitude	2.2 Willingness to Respond	→	4.1 Conceptualization of a Value
Value	2.2 Willingness to Respond	→	4.1 Conceptualization of a Value
Adjustment	2.2 Willingness to Respond	→	5.2 Characterization

Figure 7.1 Affective Progression (adapted from Krathwohl et al. 1964, 37).

actually beginning to see themselves as a certain kind of person which is aligned with the phenomenon or behavior (e.g., I am a literature or math person; I do not bully).

For those familiar with Bloom's Cognitive Taxonomy, the progression from simple order understanding (memorization) to complex knowledge (application, synthesis, evaluation), requires increasing intensity and focus. Krathwohl et al. make the same argument in regards to the affective domains. "In the cognitive domain," they content, "there is ample evidence that the lowest level of the domain—the knowledge objectives—can be achieved by a great variety of learning experiences. Basically, all that seems to be required for the development of knowledge objectives is an attentive and well-motived learner and a set of learning experiences in which an accurate version of a piece of information is communicated to the students by means of the printed page, the spoken word, or the use of pictures and illustrations" (1964, 77). Krathwohl et al. find that the same is true for the affective domain (receiving). In other words, our typical responses to bullying (teaching, giving information, training toward certain skills) can be accomplished in a number of ways (school assemblies, classroom teaching session by the school counselor, poster campaigns, communicating bullying information to staff, etc.). But, while this level of input is key, according to Krathwohl et al.'s affective taxonomy, these may alter interest, but are not sufficient to effectively foster an internalization that affects character identity (which I have argued is central to the heart change, or transformation of desire (disposition) necessary to significantly impact bullying activities). Krathwohl et al. would argue that we must move further in the taxonomy. "The more complex and higher categories of the cognitive domain require far more sophisticated learning experiences that the simple communication of a correct version of an idea or event to the student. Much more motivation is required, much more activity and participation on the part of the learner is necessary, and more opportunities must be available to help the individual to gain insight into the processes he uses as well as misuses if these more complex objectives are to be achieved. ... We believe the same principles probably apply to the affective domain" (Krathwohl et al. 1964, 77, 78).

This process of moving 'up' the taxonomy, whether in the cognitive realm (moving from memorization to the complex critical thinking necessary for the application, synthesis or evaluation of knowledge) or the affective realm (moving from awareness to conviction that affects behavior), requires concerted and sustained, even painful, effort. Krathwohl et al. conclude,

> We should point out the high cost in energy, time and commitment of achieving complex objectives in either the cognitive or the affective domain. Such objectives are not to be attained simply by someone expressing the desire that they be attained or by a few sessions of class time devoted to the attainment of the objectives. It is clear that the educators who wish to achieve these more complex objectives must be

willing to pay the rather great price entailed. . . . The point . . . is that exhortations, a rational argument for a particular behavior, and passive participation of a group of persons is likely to lead to little more than an awareness of the new material and perhaps even some intellectual conviction about the appropriateness of the new behavior. However, for any major reorganization of actual practices and responses to take place, the individual must be able to examine his own feelings and attitudes on the subject, bring them out into the open, see how they compare with the feelings and views of others, and move from an intellectual awareness of a particular behavior or practice to an actual commitment to the new practice. . . . What is suggested here, if specific changes are to take place in the learners, is that the learning experiences must be of a two-way nature in which both students and teacher are involved in an interactive manner, rather than having one resent something to be 'learned' by the other. (1964, 79, 81, 82)

Thus, like Lakatos, Krathwohl et al. argue that the process of transformation regarding the affective domain, takes more than the presentation of rational evidence to a passive 'learner.' In fact, according to Krathwohl and his colleagues, such practices are only minimally effective in the larger dispositional (attitudes, organizing value system, and internalization necessary for meaningful value and behavioral shifts). Though, like with the cognitive domain, informational approaches are foundational, we must move toward much more integrated and complex experiences to bring deeper levels of thinking or affective transformation. While Lakatos outlines core beliefs and the auxiliary theories we use to protect them (and thus help us resist transformation), Krathwohl et al. give us a framework (or a taxonomy) of what the levels of transformation might look like in the affective domain. Krathwohl and his colleagues leave us by suggesting that, "if specific changes are to take place in the learners, . . . learning experiences must be of a two-way nature in which both students and teacher are involved in an interactive manner, rather than having one resent something to be 'learned' by the other" (1964, 82). To close this chapter I turn to one final theorist, Vivian Paley, who will shed light on this process of exchange that may both subvert the auxiliary beliefs that protect the core and that may move us toward increasingly complex affective behaviors, deepening the internalization of values and attitudes. Paley's project seeks to interfere with the sacred confines of friendship, aimed at helping kindergartners allow outsiders into their intimate circles of play.

PALEY'S TRANSFORMATIONAL KINDERGARTEN

Vivian Paley, in her book *You Can't Say You Can't Play*, wants to make a simple rule to order the relationships within her class of kindergartners. But more than a simple rule, Paley is interested in the kind of moral transformation that changes disposition. "Turning sixty," she writes,

> I am more aware of the voices of exclusion in the classroom. 'You can't play' suddenly seems too overbearing and harsh, resounding like a slap from wall to wall. How casually one child determines the fate of another. 'Are you my friend/' the little ones ask in nursery school, not knowing. The responses are also questions. If yes, then what? And if I push you away, how does that feel? By kindergarten, however, a structure begins to be revealed and will soon be carved in stone. Certain children will have the right to limit the social experiences of their classmates. Henceforth a ruling class will notify others of their acceptability, and the outsiders learn to anticipate the sting of rejection. Long after hitting and name-calling have been outlawed by the teachers, a more damaging phenomenon is allowed to take root, spreading like a week from grade to grade. Must it be so? This year I am compelled to find out. Posting a sign that reads you can't say you can't play, I announce the new social order and, from the start, it is greeted with disbelief. (Paley 1992, 3)

In this project, Paley isn't as concerned about the fact that exclusion often is a part of life. Not everyone gets chosen to be an NBA basketball player and not every applicant lands the job. Exclusion, in one form or another certainly is a part of human life. Yet, the exclusion she witnesses in her classroom smacks of inequity. "Only four out of the twenty-five in my kindergarten class find the idea [i.e., the rule that if someone want to play in your game you have to let them] appealing, and they are the children most often rejected. The loudest in opposition are those who do the most rejecting. But everyone looks doubtful in the face of this unaccountable innovation. What can I possibly mean, they wonder. Is there really to be unlimited social access into their private activities? What will happen to friendship? 'But then what's the whole point of playing?' Lisa wails" (1992, 4). It is the fact that the same children get excluded again and again that bothers Paley. But, for an adult (or anyone for that matter), to dictate who your friends are becomes problematic. Why might that be? As an adult I can certainly post a 'no weapons' rule at school. I would argue that that is because it is already a part of our social story; as are any number of other intrusions into our private lives (e.g., speed limits, gender or racial discrimination, drug laws, etc.). But, regulating friendship certainly is not a part of our social norms. Perhaps parents can make demands on their younger children, but teachers or other adults cannot tell us who to be friends with. Yet, Paley notices that 'certain children' have the right (or power) to dictate the 'acceptability' of others; and those they reject are most often repeatedly rejected by others. Paley, tired of this scenario, wants to work toward a transformation of heart, or disposition, not only making a new rule (you can't say you can't

Re-Storying a School 97

play), but working to internalize such a rule, or disposition, within her students. To be honest, this is not unlike our conversation on bullying; we not only want to make a 'no bullying' rule, we want it to be internalized by all in our schools so that they desire to live according to such a code. Paley's process, then, helps shed light on such inward transformation.

Paley begins this process, not by posting the new rule, but through raising its possibility and then beginning a conversation. She begins talking with her kindergartners about what such a rule would involve. Then, she begins the same conversation with each grade level within the school. First, she discusses the possibilities with first-graders, then moves on to second-graders, etc. until she's talked with large groups of students (kindergarten through fifth grade) over the course of several months. "Several fifth graders inform me at the start," Paley recalls, "that my plan might work but not without difficulty. 'It would take a lot of getting used to,' says a girl named Rachel, 'but it could happen. Right now there's a lot of saying no but if you keep at it a long time you could get it into your brain to say yes.'" (1992, 99). This particular conversation continues:

> "Sometimes you don't want to say yes," another girl protests. "Like if I'm playing catch with my dad in the part and a kid is walking home from school and wants to play, my dad might say no, because it doesn't feel right." "It's a private time with you and your dad, "I suggest. "Right. And sometimes you have times like that with your friends." "No one would argue about the privacy of those occasions," I say. "But does the classroom qualify as a private or public?" A boy answers. "If he or she is your good friend you can always invite them to your house. So, no, this isn't a private place. It's probably a good rule but it would take years to get used to. You really do have to start in kindergarten. I can still remember kids telling me to go away in kindergarten. I remember a lot of things that happened in school when I was young, most of it not good." "Wait a minute," the boy next to him says. "in your whole life you're not going to go through life never being excluded. So you may as well learn it now. Kids are going to get in the habit of thinking they're not going to be excluded so much and it isn't true." "Maybe our classrooms can be nicer than the outside world," I say. "But this way you won't get down on yourself when you do get excluded," he insists. "Okay, but, as a teacher, here's what troubles me. Too often it's the same children, year after year, who bear the burden of rejection. They're mad to feel like strangers." (1992, 99–100)

I include this rather long piece of dialogue to give an example of the depth and nature of the conversations that Paley initiates with students in literally every grade level in her school. As we consider the 'protests' of these fifth-graders, we find ourselves thinking, "good point." In fact, throughout these conversations, kindergartners as well as fifth-graders raise legitimate concerns, talking about deep hurts, the role of 'bosses' (i.e., kids who lead or influence others) in schools, the possibility of troubling scenarios (e.g., someone wanting to play with you who isn't kind or who may even be 'dangerous'), the different rules for private and public spaces, etc. Interestingly, as evident in the above excerpt, Paley certainly pushes back, but seldom offers a definitive, rational correction or answer. She allows the questions to be asked and has the wisdom to realize that simple, one-size-fits-all answers often just don't cut it. But, shouldn't Paley be working hard to convince these children of the validity of her new rule? What is the value of simply fielding objections? We see a glimpse of Paley strategy in her conversation with a group of third graders.

> The next day, at rug time, I tell the children [i.e., her kindergartners] about the third grade discussion. "They talked about two sad children in their class, a boy and a girl." "Why are they sad?" Clara asks. "Because no one wants to play with them. They don't want the boy on their baseball teams and they don't want the girl to be their computer partner or sit with them at lunch." Angelo knows why. "They don't like those kids." The children look at me, waiting for more of an explanation. "I think the third graders feel bad about not being kinder. That's why they talked about it so much. Anyway, these two children were not completely discouraged. The boy said, 'Your plan will work if we could all get along with each other.' And the girl said, 'Sometimes people are very nice to each other, even to me.'" "What plan?" Jennifer asks. "You can't say you can't play," I remind her. "It's not our plan yet. Or, rather, it's a plan but not a rule. We're planning for it. We're talking about it getting opinions, thinking about it, wondering how it will work. I think that's a good way to start a new plan, if you've been doing something different all along." (1992, 56)

Paley's plan aimed at effective 'moral transformation' involves 'getting opinions, thinking about it, wondering how it will work,' etc. "Fortunately," Paley confides earlier to her readers, "the human species does not live by debate alone. There is an alternate route, proceeding less directly, but often better able to reach the soul of a controversy. It is story, the children's preferred frame of reference" (1992, 4). In these conversations Paley is working to internalize a new story into the hearts and minds of her students. She's not just telling them a story, though that is certainly a part of the process.[3] But, through broaching the possibility of a new rule, then engaging students in the experience of story and conversation over a long period of discussion, listening to, but never rationalizing away their concerns, Paley is beginning to build an environment where (or as Dewey would say, providing an experience where) like-mindedness can be fostered. Lakatos' auxiliary belt (e.g., but that's not how friendships work, but what if a mean person wants to play, etc.) can be deconstructed in the space of honest, conflicted dialogue.

Paley listens, and helps her students to listen, until the new evidence can begin to resonate. In a sense, in these conversations, a process of ever deepening internalization begins to happen. As Blasi would argue, in this internalization identity begins to shift; students (and Paley herself) begin to see themselves and schools differently. Another extended part of the story will be helpful here, both illustrating the nature of the dialogue I am depicting, but more importantly fleshing out the 'aim' of Paley's project:

> A boy who had been in my class tells me, "It's hard for that rule you made up to work because, see, there could be more fights, not less fights. See, if someone says you can't play and then there is a rule, so they begin to fight about the rule." "And if there's no rule?" I ask. "Then the person just walks away. That's better." "But I don't understand the rule," a girl complains. "Like what if I only want two sisters and then more people come and more people and more and it's so confusing." "That would be confusing," I admit. "Has this ever happened, where so many children wanted to play in your game?" "No,' she answers simply. "But what if it was someone mean you didn't like?" There is a moment of silence while we all contemplate the intrusion of strange and unwanted people into our intimate games. During the pause I tell the children a true story. "Some of you know Mrs. Wilson, who teaches with me. Her building shares a backyard with two other buildings. All the children in all the buildings play in that one yard and they follow a simple rule: *Everyone can play*. When a child comes out the older ones ask, 'Do you want to play?' And if someone is mean or fights a lot they tell him or her not to do it and they keep saying it until the child remembers to play nicely." The children are fascinated by my story. "What do you think of Mrs. Wilson's backyard?" I ask. "It's very nice." "Those are really nice kids." "I wish I lived there." "So do I," I say. "Could this happen in a classroom?" Maybe," says the boy who worried about my rule causing more fighting. "It's very fair. But people aren't that fair as the rule is." (1992, 35, 36)

Again, we see the back and forth dialogue. Of course, remembering back to Bloom's affective taxonomy, dialogue without an openness to listen, simply is not dialogue. The given here is that the topic is relevant to all involved and an openness in that dialogue is strong enough, that the conversation truly becomes reciprocal (teacher/students working together on a compelling problem). But, we also notice here what Paley is shooting for. In Mrs. Wilson's back yard there are no adults monitoring and enforcing the 'everyone can play' rule. The older students are monitoring. Now these students are not paid security guards; they monitor because they have 'bought into' the rule. Paley isn't working only toward compliance in her classroom. Instead, she is aiming at creating certain kinds of people, with certain kinds of dispositions that for the rest of their lives will carry with them inclusive attitudes. This is not classroom management, this is dispositional transformation; this is Dewey's moral education.

Lisa, who Paley acknowledges has the most to lose when the new rule is adopted, serves as its loudest critic. After several months of conversation, Paley finally posts the new rule on the classroom wall. Even though all are well-versed in the implications, the actual transition demands a shift in mindset; this is certainly true for Lisa. "'It' not fair at all.' Lisa pouts. 'I thought we were only just talking about it. I just want my own friends. What if someone isn't nice and hits me?'" (1994, 82). Lisa's core beliefs about friendship (i.e., outsiders shouldn't pick our friends for us, we should be able to choose our own friends) is still strongly internalized. But, as Lakatos' argues, openness to a new story is what allows one to consider new evidence and, thus, to shift. Those months of conversation had begun to create a 'like-mindedness' in Lisa that, though she still resisted, provided with a level of openness that would allow her to begin the progression along Krathwohl's taxonomy of affective growth. In a subsequent interview several years later, Paley thinks back on this year of transformation, and especially about Lisa. Paley relays that it took about a week for the new rule to settle in. After that everyone acted as if it had always been the rule. As for Lisa, Paley noted that whenever she saw Lisa in the school hallway after her kindergarten year, Lisa would ask her 'how it was going with the new rule,' then share an incident where she had tried to keep it. In fact, after Lisa left the school, Paley tells, she ran into her and her mother at a local grocery store. Lisa volunteered in the subsequent conversation that, though it was hard for her, she continued to work hard to put the rule into practice in all encounters (This American Life, 19??). For Lisa the rule had moved from one that was imposed from the outside under the watchful eye of a teacher or another adult, to a disposition that motivated Lisa whether she was being watched or not. Her attitude had shifted; she had come to see herself as a person who regularly sought to include others and she strove to live out that identity. Lakatos would say she shifted to a new 'belief.' Krathwohl et al. would say that the affective value of inclusion had come to characterize Lisa's life. And Dewey would argue that the experience that Paley provided (conversation, rule-constructing, fielding questions, etc.) had worked to create a relational like-mindedness where Lisa's heart (i.e., desire, attitude, or disposition) had been transformed. Lisa had become like one of the older students in Mrs. Wilson's backyard. Paley, through an extended period of conversation raised a new story for her students regarding friendship and inclusion; a re-storying that stuck with them long after their kindergarten year. We are now ready to consider a more nuanced response in our anti-bullying efforts within schools.

8 Toward a Holistic Anti-Bullying Model
Culture, Safety, and Moral Transformation

BACK TO THE BUMP GAME

> By kindergarten, however, a structure begins to be revealed and will soon be carved in stone. Certain children will have the right to limit the social experiences of their classmates. Henceforth a ruling class will notify others of their acceptability, and the outsiders learn to anticipate the sting of rejection. (Paley 1992, 3)

In these pages I have certainly not intended to psychoanalyze Jake or his friends. That would be an exercise in futility from this distance. I have also not meant to simplify bulling activity into a succinct one-size-fits-all phenomenon. Bullying activity is complex, nuanced and, I would argue, often escapes the understanding even of those involved in its activities. But, I have meant to use the Southside incident as a site to deeply consider the interactions surrounding typical bullying encounters. Research is clear: bullying consistently plays out in front of watching peers and often it is intractable. In other words, once a student has taken up bullying behavior it often is very difficult to make them stop.

In this project I have undertaken a focused task: I have wanted to better understand Jake's 'I like.' What might it have been that was so satisfying to Jake; so much so that he was willing to incur the disappointment of his parents, the reprimand of school administrators, and the punishments meted out by the adults surrounding him? And further, whatever Jake was 'getting' in these exchanges of dominance, why was public dominance the tool of choice for Jake at Southside? Why did the participants in the bump game so readily understand the premise of what Jake was doing and so easily join in? In other words, how might bullying become a viable pathway to secure the satisfaction that Jake sought?

I have argued that connected to Jake's 'satisfaction' was the status he received as he publically dominated Matthew in the bump game. The high-fives and knowing smiles meant that Jake was accepted and esteemed. He became somebody as he humiliated Matthew in front of his peers. I have also argued that the story of schooling is one that provides a pathway to status through dominance. One could argue that Jake had simply taken seriously the rhetoric of schooling; i.e., the one on top is the one who receives the accolades. Finally, I have argued that the 'identity' that Jake sought through dominance can only be secured in reciprocity. Thus, Jake's attempt to secure identity through dominance will always fall flat, making that need insatiable and his bullying activities continual. In the last two chapters I have more deeply considered issues of cultural stories and moral education, especially noting why such education is resistant to our anti-bullying programs, our lectures, and our punishments. In light of this discussion, I now turn to specific steps that might we take to more holistically respond to bullying activity in transformative ways. There are two important trajectories that parents, youth workers and schools must embark on simultaneously. Safety frames the first.

RESPONSE AND SAFETY

As alluded to in Chapter 2, most states now have P-12 school anti-bullying/anti-harassment laws on their books. The laws in Washington State are typical.[1]

RCW 28A.300.285: HARASSMENT, INTIMIDATION, AND BULLYING

1) By August 1, 2003, each school district shall adopt or amend if necessary a policy, within the scope of its authority, that prohibits the harassment, intimidation, or bullying of any student. It is the responsibility of each school district to share this policy with parents or guardians, students, volunteers, and school employees.
2) "Harassment, intimidation, or bullying" means any intentional electronic, written, verbal, or physical act, including but not limited to one shown to be motivated by any characteristic in RCW 9A.36.080(3), or other distinguishing characteristics, when the intentional electronic, written, verbal, or physical act:

   a) Physically harms a student or damages the student's property; or
   b) Has the effect of substantially interfering with a student's education; or
   c) Is so severe, persistent, or pervasive that it creates an intimidating or threatening educational environment; or
   d) Has the effect of substantially disrupting the orderly operation of the school.

Nothing in this section requires the affected student to actually possess a characteristic that is a basis for the harassment, intimidation, or bullying.

The policy should be adopted or amended through a process that includes representation of parents or guardians, school employees, volunteers, students, administrators, and community representatives. It is recommended that each such policy emphasize positive character traits and values, including the importance of civil and respectful speech and conduct, and the responsibility of students to comply with the district's policy prohibiting harassment, intimidation, or bullying.

4) By August 1, 2002, the superintendent of public instruction, in consultation with representatives of parents, school personnel, and other interested parties, shall provide to school districts and educational service districts a model harassment, intimidation, and bullying prevention policy and training materials on the components that should be included in any district policy. Training materials shall be disseminated in a variety of ways, including workshops and other staff developmental activities, and through the office of the superintendent of public instruction's web site, with a link to the safety center web page. On the web site:

   a) The office of the superintendent of public instruction shall post its model policy, recommended training materials, and instructional materials;
   b) The office of the superintendent of public instruction has the authority to update with new technologies access to this information in the safety center, to the extent resources are made available; and
   c) Individual school districts shall have direct access to the safety center web site to post a brief summary of their policies, programs, partnerships, vendors, and instructional and training materials, and to provide a link to the school district's web site for further information.

5) The Washington state school directors association, with the assistance of the office of the superintendent of public instruction, shall convene an advisory committee to develop a model policy prohibiting acts of harassment, intimidation, or bullying that are conducted via electronic means by a student while on school grounds and during the school day. The policy shall include a requirement that materials meant to educate parents and students about the seriousness of cyberbullying be disseminated to parents or made available on the school district's web site. The school directors association and the advisory committee shall develop sample materials for school districts to disseminate, which shall also include information on responsible and safe internet use as well as what options are available if a student is being bullied via electronic means, including but not limited to, reporting threats to local police and when to involve school officials,

6) the internet service provider, or phone service provider. The school directors association shall submit the model policy and sample materials, along with a recommendation for local adoption, to the governor and the legislature and shall post the model policy and sample materials on its web site by January 1, 2008. Each school district board of directors shall establish its own policy by August 1, 2008.
6) As used in this section, "electronic" or "electronic means" means any communication where there is the transmission of information by wire, radio, optical cable, electromagnetic, or other similar means (http://apps.leg.wa.gov/documents/billdocs/2009-10/Pdf/Bills/House%20Passed%20Legislature/2801-S.PL.pdf).

State law is the starting point for anti-bullying policy and programs.[2] This is especially important in regards to the safety of all students within the school. The legal piece is foundational to any response. Parents, teachers, administrators, and even students should become familiar with their state's anti-bullying laws, understanding the definitions and consequences involved. From such laws, states, school districts, and individual schools must then develop policies and procedures regarding bullying activities.

Based on these laws, the next step regarding safety is to create district or school policy. Again, drawing on documents available in Washington State from the Office of the Superintendent of Public Instruction (http://www.k12.wa.us/SafetyCenter/BullyingHarassment), policies should be straightforward and all-encompassing.

PROHIBITION OF HARASSMENT, INTIMIDATION, AND BULLYING

The district is committed to a safe and civil educational environment for all students, employees, parents/legal guardians, volunteers, and patrons that is free from harassment, intimidation, or bullying. "Harassment, intimidation, or bullying" means any intentionally written message or image—including those that are electronically transmitted—verbal, or physical act, including but not limited to one shown to be motivated by race, color, religion, ancestry, national origin, gender, sexual orientation, including gender expression or identity, mental or physical disability or other distinguishing characteristics, when an act:

- Physically harms a student or damages the student's property.
- Has the effect of substantially interfering with a student's education.
- Is so severe, persistent or pervasive that it creates an intimidating or threatening educational environment.
- Has the effect of substantially disrupting the orderly operation of the school.

Nothing in this section requires the affected student to actually possess a characteristic that is a basis for the harassment, intimidation, or bullying.

"Other distinguishing characteristics" can include but are not limited to: physical appearance, clothing or other apparel, socioeconomic status, and weight.

"Intentional acts" refers to the individual's choice to engage in the act rather than the ultimate impact of the action(s).

Behaviors/Expressions

Harassment, intimidation, or bullying can take many forms including, but not limited to slurs, rumors, jokes, innuendos, demeaning comments, drawings, cartoons, pranks, gestures, physical attacks, threats or other written, oral, physical, or electronically transmitted messages or images.

This policy is not intended to prohibit expression of religious, philosophical, or political views, provided that the expression does not substantially disrupt the educational environment. Many behaviors that do not rise to the level of harassment, intimidation, or bullying may still be prohibited by other district policies or building, classroom, or program rules.

Training

This policy is a component of the district's responsibility to create and maintain a safe, civil, respectful, and inclusive learning community and shall be implemented in conjunction with comprehensive training of students, staff and volunteers.

Prevention

The district will provide students with strategies aimed at preventing harassment, intimidation, and bullying. In its efforts to train students, the district will seek partnerships with families, law enforcement, and other community agencies.

Interventions

Interventions are designed to remediate the impact on the targeted student(s) and others impacted by the violation, to change the behavior of the perpetrator, and to restore a positive school climate.

The district will consider the frequency of incidents, developmental age of the student, and severity of the conduct in determining intervention strategies. Interventions will range from counseling, correcting behavior and discipline, to law enforcement referrals.

Retaliation/False Allegations

Retaliation is prohibited and will result in appropriate discipline. It is a violation of this policy to threaten or harm someone for reporting harassment, intimidation, or bullying.

It is also a violation of district policy to knowingly report false allegations of harassment, intimidation, and bullying. Students or employees will not be disciplined for making a report in good faith. However, persons found to knowingly report or corroborate false allegations will be subject to appropriate discipline.

Compliance Officer

The superintendent will appoint a compliance officer as the primary district contact to receive copies of all formal and informal complaints and ensure policy implementation. The name and contact information for the compliance officer will be communicated throughout the district.

The superintendent is authorized to direct the implementation of procedures addressing the elements of this policy.

Cross References:	Policy 3200	Rights and Responsibilities
	Policy 3210	Nondiscrimination
	Policy 3240	Student Conduct
	Policy 3241	Classroom Management, Corrective Action and Punishment
	Policy 6590	Sexual Harassment
Legal Reference:	RCW 28A.300.285	Harassment, intimidation, and bullying prevention policies
	RCW 28A.600.480	Reporting of harassment, intimidation, or bullying—Retaliation prohibited—Immunity
	RCW 9A.36.080	Malicious Harassment—Definition and criminal penalty
	RCW 28A.642	K-12 Education—Prohibition of discrimination
	RCW 49.60	Discrimination—Human Rights Commission

U.S. Depart. of Education, Dear Colleague Letter, 2010. http://www2.ed.gov/about/offices/list/ocr/letters/colleague-201010.html

(2012 OSPI website)

MICHIGAN STATE BOARD OF EDUCATION

Model Anti-Bullying Policy

The (fill in district name) board of education recognizes that a school that is physically and emotionally safe and secure for all students promotes good citizenship, increases student attendance and engagement, and supports academic achievement. To protect the rights of all students and groups for a safe and secure learning environment, the board of education prohibits acts of bullying, harassment, and other forms of aggression and violence. Bullying or harassment, like other forms of aggressive and violent behaviors, interferes with both a school's ability to educate its students and a student's ability to learn. All administrators, faculty, staff, parents, volunteers, and students are expected to refuse to tolerate bullying and harassment and to demonstrate behavior that is respectful and civil. It is especially important for adults to model these behaviors (even when disciplining) in order to provide positive examples for student behavior.

"Bullying" or "harassment" is any gesture or written, verbal, graphic, or physical act (including electronically transmitted acts—i.e., cyberbullying, through the use of internet, cell phone, personal digital assistant (pda), computer, or wireless handheld device, currently in use or later developed and used by students) that is reasonably perceived as being dehumanizing, intimidating, hostile, humiliating, threatening, or otherwise likely to evoke fear of physical harm or emotional distress and may be motivated either by bias or prejudice based upon any actual or perceived characteristic, such as race, color, religion, ancestry, national origin, gender, sexual orientation, gender identity or expression; or a mental, physical, or sensory disability or impairment; or by any other distinguishing characteristic, or is based upon association with another person who has or is perceived to have any distinguishing characteristic. Bullying and harassment also include forms of retaliation against individuals who report or cooperate in an investigation under this policy. Such behaviors are considered to be bullying or harassment whether they take place on or off school property, at any school-sponsored function, or in a school vehicle or at any time or place where a child's imminent safety or over-all well being may be at issue.

"Bullying" is conduct that meets all of the following criteria:

- is reasonably perceived as being dehumanizing, intimidating, hostile, humiliating, threatening, or otherwise likely to evoke fear of physical harm or emotional distress;
- is directed at one or more pupils;
- is conveyed through physical, verbal, technological or emotional means;

- substantially interferes with educational opportunities, benefits, or programs of one or more pupils;
- adversely affects the ability of a pupil to participate in or benefit from the school district's or public school's educational programs or activities by placing the pupil in reasonable fear of physical harm or by causing emotional distress; and,
- is based on a pupil's actual or perceived distinguishing characteristic (see above), or is based on an association with another person who has or is perceived to have any of these characteristics.

"Harassment" is conduct that meets all of the following criteria:

- is reasonably perceived as being dehumanizing, intimidating, hostile, humiliating, threatening, or otherwise likely to evoke fear of physical harm or emotional distress;
- is directed at one or more pupils;
- is conveyed through physical, verbal, technological or emotional means;
- substantially interferes with educational opportunities, benefits, or programs of one or more pupils;
- adversely affects the ability of a pupil to participate in or benefit from the school district's or public school's educational programs or activities because the conduct, as reasonably perceived by the pupil, is so severe, pervasive, and objectively offensive as to have this effect; and,
- is based on a pupil's actual or perceived distinguishing characteristic (see above), or is based on an association with another person who has or is perceived to have any of these characteristics.

The scope of this policy includes the prohibition of every form of bullying, harassment, and cyberbullying/harassment, whether in the classroom, on school premises, immediately adjacent to school premises, when a student is traveling to or from school (portal to portal), or at a school-sponsored event, whether or not held on school premises. Bullying or harassment, including cyberbullying/ harassment, that is not initiated at a location defined above is covered by this policy if the incident results in a potentially material or substantial disruption of the school learning environment for one or more students and/or the orderly day-to-day operations of any school or school program.

The (fill in district name) board of education expects students to conduct themselves in a manner in keeping with their levels of development, maturity, and demonstrated capabilities with a proper regard for the rights and welfare of other students, school staff, volunteers, and contractors (Michigan State Department of Education).

An additional Washington State OSPI 'Threat Policy' touches on communication issues/responsibilities:

POLICY STATEMENT: NOTIFICATION OF THREATS OF VIOLENCE OR HARM

Students and school employees who are subjects of threats of violence or harm shall be notified of the threats in a timely manner. Parents shall be included in notifications to students who are subjects of threats of violence or harm. Timing and details of the notice will be as extensive as permitted by the federal Family Educational Rights and Privacy Act, other legal limitations, and the circumstances.

Individual-directed threats of violence or harm are communications that create fear of physical harm to a specific individual or individuals, communicated directly or indirectly by any means.

Building-directed threats of violence or harm are direct or indirect communications by any means of the intent to cause damage to a school building or school property (e.g., bomb threats), or to harm students, employees, volunteers, patrons or visitors.

The district will address threats of violence or harm in a manner consistent with the district's safety policies and comprehensive safe school plans.

Persons found to have made threats of violence or harm against district property, students, employees or others will be subject to relevant district discipline policies and will be referred to appropriate community agencies including law enforcement and mental health services. District staff shall work with in-district and community-based professionals and services in all relevant disciplines to address threats of violence or harm, those threatened and those making the threats. Necessary information about the person making the threat shall be communicated by the principal to teachers and staff, including security personnel.

State law provides the district, school district directors and district staff with immunity from liability for providing notice of threats in good faith. Persons who make a knowingly false notification of a threat are subject to appropriate district discipline policies and may be referred for prosecution.

The superintendent is directed to develop and implement procedures consistent with this policy (2012 OSPI website).

Once policies are in place, it is important to develop specific procedures regarding what students, teachers, and parents should do when bullying does occur. Again, leaning on the OSPI website, it is important to lay out steps to take, including forms and contact points:

PROHIBITION OF HARASSMENT, INTIMIDATION, AND BULLYING

A. Introduction

_____School District strives to provide students with optimal conditions for learning by maintaining a school environment where everyone is treated with respect and no one is physically or emotionally harmed.

In order to ensure respect and prevent harm, it is a violation of district policy for a student to be harassed, intimidated, or bullied by others in the school community, at school sponsored events, or when such actions create a substantial disruption to the educational process. The school community includes all students, school employees, school board members, contractors, unpaid volunteers, families, patrons, and other visitors. Student(s) will not be harassed because of their race, color, religion, ancestry, national origin, gender, sexual orientation, including gender expression or identity, mental or physical disability, or other distinguishing characteristics.

Any school staff who observes, overhears, or otherwise witnesses harassment, intimidation, or bullying or to whom such actions have been reported must take prompt and appropriate action to stop the harassment and to prevent its reoccurrence.

B. Definitions

Aggressor—is a student, staff member, or other member of the school community who engages in the harassment, intimidation, or bullying of a student.

Harassment, intimidation, or bullying—is an intentional electronic, written, verbal, or physical act that:

> Physically harms a student or damages the student's property.
> Has the effect of substantially interfering with a student's education.
> Is so severe, persistent, or pervasive that it creates an intimidating or threatening educational environment.
> Has the effect of substantially disrupting the orderly operation of the school.

Conduct that is "substantially interfering with a student's education" will be determined by considering a targeted student's grades, attendance, demeanor, interaction with peers, participation in activities, and other indicators.

Conduct that may rise to the level of harassment, intimidation, and bullying may take many forms, including, but not limited to, slurs, rumors, jokes, innuendoes, demeaning comments, drawings, cartoons, pranks, ostracism, physical attacks or threats, gestures, or acts relating to an individual or group whether electronic, written, oral, or physically transmitted messages or images. There is no requirement that the targeted student actually possess the characteristic that is the basis for the harassment, intimidation, or bullying.

Incident Reporting Form—may be used by students, families, or staff to report incidents of harassment, intimidation, or bullying. A sample form is provided on the Office of Superintendent of Public Instruction's (OSPI)

School Safety Center Web site: http://www.k12.wa.us/SafetyCenter/BullyingHarassment/default.aspx.
Retaliation—when an aggressor harasses, intimidates, or bullies a student who has reported incidents of bullying.
Staff—includes, but is not limited to, educators, administrators, counselors, school nurses, cafeteria workers, custodians, bus drivers, athletic coaches, advisors to extracurricular activities, classified staff, substitute and temporary teachers, volunteers, or paraprofessionals (both employees and contractors).
Targeted Student—is a student against whom harassment, intimidation, or bullying has allegedly been perpetrated.

C. Relationship to Other Laws

This procedure applies only to RCW 28A.300.285—Harassment, Intimidation and Bullying prevention. There are other laws and procedures to address related issues such as sexual harassment or discrimination.

At least four Washington laws may apply to harassment or discrimination:

- RCW 28A.300.285—12 Education—Harassment, Intimidation and Bullying
- RCW 28A.640.020—Sexual Harassment
- RCW 28A.642—Prohibition of Discrimination in Public Schools
- RCW 49.60.010—The Law Against Discrimination

The district will ensure its compliance with all state laws regarding harassment, intimidation or bullying. Nothing in this procedure prevents a student, parent/guardian, school or district from taking action to remediate harassment or discrimination based on a person's gender or membership in a legally protected class under local, state, or federal law.

D. Prevention

1. Dissemination
   In each school and on the district's Web site the district will prominently post information on reporting harassment, intimidation, and bullying; the name and contact information for making a report to a school administrator; and the name and contact information for the district compliance officer. The district's policy and procedure will be available in each school in a language that families can understand.

   Annually, the superintendent will ensure that a statement summarizing the policy and procedure is provided in student, staff, volunteer, and parent handbooks, is available in school and district offices and/or hallways, or is posted on the district's Web site.

Additional distribution of the policy and procedure is subject to the requirements of Washington Adminstrative Code 392–400–226.

2. Education
Annually students will receive age-appropriate information on the recognition and prevention of harassment, intimidation, or bullying at student orientation sessions and on other appropriate occasions. The information will include a copy of the Incident Reporting Form or a link to a Web-based form.

3. Training
Staff will receive annual training on the school district's policy and procedure, including staff roles and responsibilities, how to monitor common area, and the use of the district's Incident Reporting Form.

4. Prevention Strategies
The district will implement a range of prevention strategies including individual, classroom, school, and district-level approaches.

Whenever possible, the district will implement evidence-based prevention programs that are designed to increase social competency, improve school climate, and eliminate harassment, intimidation, and bullying in schools.

E. Compliance Officer

The district compliance officer will:

1. Serve as the district's primary contact for harassment, intimidation, and bullying.
2. Provide support and assistance to the principal or designee in resolving complaints.
3. Receive copies of all Incident Reporting Forms, discipline Referral Forms, and letters to parents providing the outcomes of investigations.
4. Be familiar with the use of the student information system. The compliance officer may use this information to identify patterns of behavior and areas of concern.
5. Ensure implementation of the policy and procedure by overseeing the investigative processes, including ensuring that investigations are prompt, impartial, and thorough.

6. Assess the training needs of staff and students to ensure successful implementation throughout the district, and ensure staff receive annual fall training.
7. Provide the OSPI School Safety Center with notification of policy or procedure updates or changes on an annual basis.
8. In cases where, despite school efforts, a targeted student experiences harassment, intimidation, or bullying that threatens the student's health and safety, the compliance officer will facilitate a meeting between district staff and the child's parents/guardians to develop a safety plan to protect the student. A sample student safety plan is available on the OSPI Web site: *http://www.k12.wa.us/SafetyCenter/default.aspx.*

F. Staff Intervention

All staff members shall intervene when witnessing or receiving reports of harassment, intimdidation or bullying. Minor incidents that staff are able to resolve immediately, or incidents that do not meet the definition of harassment, intimidation, or bullying, may require no further action under this procedure.

G. Filing an Incident Reporting Form

Any student who believes he or she has been the target of unresolved, severe, or persistent harassment, intimidation, or bullying, or any other person in the school community who observes or receives notice that a student has or may have been the target of unresolved, severe, or persistent harassment, intimidation, or bullying, may report incidents verbally or in writing to any staff member.

H. Addressing Bullying—Reports

Step 1: Filing an Incident Reporting Form

In order to protect a targeted student from retaliation, a student need not reveal his identity on an Incident Reporting Form. The form may be filed anonymously, confidentially, or the student may choose to disclose his or her identity (non-confidential).
Status of Reporter

   a. Anonymous
   Individuals may file a report without revealing their identity. No disciplinary action will be taken against an alleged aggressor based solely on an anonymous report. Schools may identify complaint boxes or develop other methods for receiving anonymous, unsigned

reports. Possible responses to an anonymous report include enhanced monitoring of specific locations at certain times of day or increased monitoring of specific students or staff. (Example: An unsigned Incident Reporting Form dropped on a teacher's desk led to the increased monitoring of the boys' locker room in 5th period.)

b. Confidential
Individuals may ask that their identities be kept secret from the accused and other students. Like anonymous reports, no disciplinary action will be taken against an alleged aggressor based solely on a confidential report. (Example: A student tells a playground supervisor about a classmate being bullied but asks that nobody know who reported the incident. The supervisor says, "I won't be able to punish the bullies unless you or someone else who saw it is willing to let me use their names, but I can start hanging out near the basketball court, if that would help.")

c. Non-confidential
Individuals may agree to file a report non-confidentially. Complainants agreeing to make their complaint non-confidential will be informed that due process requirements may require that the district release all of the information that it has regarding the complaint to any individuals involved in the incident, but that even then, information will still be restricted to those with a need to know, both during and after the investigation. The district will, however, fully implement the anti-retaliation provision of this policy and procedure to protect complainants and witnesses.

Step 2: Receiving an Incident Reporting Form

All staff are responsible for receiving oral and written reports. Whenever possible staff who initially receive an oral or written report of harassment, intimidation, or bullying shall attempt to resolve the incident immediately. If the incident is resolved to the satisfaction of the parties involved, or if the incident does not meet the definition of harassment, intimidation, or bullying, no further action may be necessary under this procedure.

All reports of unresolved, severe, or persistent harassment, intimidation, or bullying will be recorded on a district Incident Reporting Form and submitted to the principal or designee, unless the designee is the subject of the complaint.

Step 3: Investigations of Unresolved, Severe, or Persistent Harassment, Intimidation and Bullying

All reports of unresolved, severe, or persistent harassment, intimidation, or bullying will be investigated with resonable promptness. Any student may have a trusted adult with them throughout the report and investigation process.

   a. Upon receipt of the Incident Reporting Form that alleges unresolved, severe, or persistent harassment, intimidation or bullying, the school or district designee will begin the investigation. If there is potential for clear and immediate physical harm to the complainant, the district will immediately contact law enforcement and inform the parent/guardian.

   b. During the course of the investigation, the district will take reasonable measures to ensure that no further incidents of harassment, intimidation, or bullying occur between the complainant and the alleged aggressor. If necessary, the district will implement a safety plan for the student(s) involved. The plan may include changing seating arrangements for the complainant and/or the alleged aggressor in the classroom, at lunch, or on the bus; identifying a staff member who will act as a safe person for the complainant; altering the alleged agressor's schedule and access to the complainant, and other measures.

   c. Within two (2) school days after receiving the Incident Reporting Form, the school designee will notify the families of the students involved that a complaint was received and direct the families to the district's policy and procedure on harassment, intimidation, and bullying.

   d. In rare cases, where after consultation with the student and appropriate staff (such as a psychologist, counselor, or social worker) the district has evidence that it would threaten the health and safety of the complainant or the alleged aggressor to involve his or her parent/guardian, the district may initially refrain from contacting the parent/guardian in its investigation of harassment, intimidation, and bullying. If professional school personnel suspect that a student is subject to abuse and neglect, they must follow district policy for reporting suspected cases to Child Protective Services.

   e. The investigation shall include, at a minimum:

   - An interview with the complainant.
   - An interview with the alleged aggressor.
   - A review of any previous complaints involving either the complainant or the alleged aggressor.
   - Interviews with other students or staff members who may have knowledge of the alleged incident.

   f. The principal or designee may determine that other steps must be taken before the investigation is complete.

g. The investigation will be completed as soon as practicable but generally no later than five (5) school days from the initial complaint or report. If more time is needed to complete an investigation, the district will provide the parent/guardian and/or the student with weekly updates.

h. No later than two (2) school days after the investigation has been completed and submitted to the compliance officer, the principal or designee shall respond in writing or in person to the parent/guardian of the complainant and the alleged aggressor stating:

- The results of the investigation.
- Whether the allegations were found to be factual.
- Whether there was a violation of policy.
- The process for the complainant to file an appeal if the complainant disagrees with results.

Because of the legal requirement regarding the confidentiality of student records, the principal or designee may not be able to report specific information to the targeted student's parent/guardian about any disciplinary action taken unless it involves a directive that the targeted student must be aware of in order to report violations.

If a district chooses to contact the parent/guardian by letter, the letter will be mailed to the parent/guardian of the complainant and alleged aggressor by United States postal service with return receipt requested unless it is determined, after consultation with the student and appropriate staff (psychologist, counselor, social worker) that it could endanger the complainant or the alleged aggressor to involve his or her family. If professional school personnel suspect that a student is subject to abuse or neglect, as mandatory reporters they must follow district policy for reporting suspected cases to Child Protective Services.

If the incident is unable to be resolved at the school level, the principal or designee shall request assistance from the district.

Step 4: Corrective Measures for the Aggressor

After completion of the investigation, the school or district designee will institute any corrective measures necessary. Corrective measures will be instituted as quickly as possible, but in no event more than five (5) school days after contact has been made to the families or guardians regarding the outcome of the investigation. Corrective measures that involve student discipline will be implemented according to district policy XXXX—student discipline. If the accused aggressor is appealing the imposition of discipline, the district may be prevented by due process considerations or a lawful order from imposing the discipline until the appeal process is concluded.

If in an investigation a principal or principal's designee found that a student knowingly made a false allegation of harassment, intimidation, or bullying, that student may be subject to corrective measures, including discipline.

Step 5: Targeted Student's Right to Appeal

1. If the complainant or parent/guardian is dissatisfied with the results of the investigation, they may appeal to the superintendent or his or her designee by filing a written notice of appeal within five (5) school days of receiving the written decision. The superintendent or his or her designee will review the investigative report and issue a written decision on the merits of the appeal within five (5) school days of receiving the notice of appeal.
2. If the targeted student remains dissatisfied after the initial appeal to the superintendent, the student may appeal to the school board by filing a written notice of appeal with the secretary of the school board on or before the *fifth* (5) school day following the date upon which the complainant received the superintendent's written decision.
3. An appeal before the school board or disciplinary appeal council must be heard on or before the tenth (10) school day following the filing of the written notice of appeal to the school board. The school board or disciplinary appeal council will review the record and render a written decision on the merits of the appeal on or before the fifth (5) school day following the termination of the hearing, and shall provide a copy to all parties involved. The board or council's decision will be the final district decision.

Step 6: Discipline/Corrective Action

The district will take prompt and equitable corrective measures within its authority on findings of harassment, intimidation, or bullying. Depending on the severity of the conduct, corrective measures may include counseling, education, discipline, and/or referral to law enforcement.

Corrective measures for a student who commits an act of harassment, intimidation, or bullying will be varied and graded according to the nature of the behavior, the developmental age of the student, or the student's history of problem behaviors and performance. Corrective measures that involve student discipline will be implemented according to district policy XXXX—student discipline.

118   Rethinking School Bullying

If the conduct was of a public nature or involved groups of students or bystanders, the district should strongly consider schoolwide training or other activities to address the incident.

If staff have been found to be in violation of this policy and procedure, school districts may impose employment disciplinary action, up to and including termination. If a certificated educator is found to have committed a violation of WAC 181–87, commonly called the Code of Conduct for Professional Educators, OSPI's Office of Professional Practices may propose disciplinary action on a certificate, up to and including revocation. Contractor violations of this policy may include the loss of contracts.

Step 7: Support for the Targeted Student

Persons found to have been subjected to harassment, intimidation, or bullying will have appropriate district support services made available to them, and the adverse impact of the harassment on the student shall be addressed and remedied as appropriate.

I. Immunity/Retaliation

No school employee, student, or volunteer may engage in reprisal or retaliation against a targeted student, witness, or other person who brings forward information about an alleged act of harassment, intimidation, or bullying. Retaliation is prohibited and will result in appropriate discipline.

J. Other Resources

Students and families should use the district's complaint and appeal procedures as a first response to allegations of harassment, intimidation, and bullying. However, nothing in this procedure prevents a student, parent/guardian, school, or district from taking action to remediate discrimination or harassment based on a person's membership in a legally protected class under local, state or federal law. An harassment, intimidation, or bullying complaint may also be reported to the following state or federal agencies:

- OSPI Equity and Civil Rights Office (360) 725–6162
  Email: equity@k12.wa.us
  www.k12.wa.us/Equity/default.aspx

- Washington State Human Rights Commission
  1 (800) 233–3247
  www.hum.wa.gov/index.html

- Office for Civil Rights, U.S. Department of Education, Region IX
  (206) 607-1600
  Email: OCR.Seattle@ed.gov
  www.ed.gov/about/offices/list/ocr/index.html

- Department of Justice Community Relations Service
  1 (877) 292-3804
  www.justice.gov/crt/

- Office of the Education Ombudsman
  1 (866) 297-2597
  Email: OEOinfo@gov.wa.gov
  www.governor.wa.gov/oeo/default.asp

- OSPI Safety Center
  (360) 725-6044
  http://www.k12.wa.us/SafetyCenter/BullyingHarassment/default.aspx

K. Other District Policies and Procedures

Nothing in this policy or procedure is intended to prohibit discipline or remedial action for inappropriate behaviors that do not rise to the level of harassment, intimidation, or bullying as defined herein, but which are, or may be, prohibited by other district or school rules (http://www.k12.wa.us/SafetyCenter/Guidance/pubdocs/Anti-BullyingProcedureFinal.pdf).

**Washington State Harassment, Intimidation or Bullying (HIB)
Sample Incident Reporting Form**

Reporting person (optional): _____

Targeted student: _____

Your email address (optional): _____

Your phone number (optional): _____ Today's date: _____

Name of school adult you've already contacted (if any): _____

Name(s) of bullies (if known): _____

On what dates did the incident(s) happen (if known): _____

Where did the incident happen? Circle all that apply.

Classroom	Hallway	Restroom	Playground	Locker room	Lunchroom
Sport field	Parking lot	School bus	Internet	Cell phone	During a school activity

120 Rethinking School Bullying

Off school property   On the way to/from school

Other (Please describe): _____

Please check the box that best describes what the bully did. Please choose all that apply.

- ☐ Hitting, kicking, shoving, spitting, hair pulling or throwing something at the student
- ☐ Getting another person to hit or harm the student
- ☐ Teasing, name calling, making critical remarks or threatening in person, by phone, by e-mail, etc.
- ☐ Putting the student down and making the student a target of jokes
- ☐ Making rude and/or threatening gestures
- ☐ Excluding or rejecting the student
- ☐ Making the student fearful, demanding money or exploiting
- ☐ Spreading harmful rumors or gossip
- ☐ Cyber bullying (bullying by calling, texting, emailing, web posting, etc.)
- ☐ Other

If you select other, please describe: _____

Why do you think the harassment, intimidation or bullying occurred? _____

_____

Were there any witnesses? Yes ☐ No ☐ If yes, please provide their names: _____

_____

Did a physical injury result from this incident? If yes, please describe. _____

_____

Was the target absent from school as a result of the incident? Yes ☐ No ☐ If yes, please describe.

_____

_____

Is there any additional information? _____

_____

Thank you for reporting!

_____

For Office Use

Received by: _____

Date received: _____

Action taken: _____

_____

Parent/guardian contacted: _____

Circle one: Resolved   Unresolved

                Referred to: _____

HARASSMENT, INTIMIDATION OR BULLYING—TARGETED STUDENT SAFETY PLAN TEMPLATE

Definitions and Guidance:

Our school provides a safe and secure learning environment that is free from of **harassment, intimidation or bullying (HIB)**. Especially vulnerable students who have been the **alleged targets** of HIB may need special protection to ensure their emotional and physical safety is secure during investigations and/or after sanctions have been imposed on aggressor students.

This safety plan template raises key issues for you to consider to assist in the protection of a vulnerable student and in the writing of a safety plan. It is understood that each situation is different and that additional considerations may be included.

It is recommended that this **Student Safety Plan** be completed by the school's **existing safety, discipline or student support team.** Examples of such groups include a school's Care Team, Student Intervention Team (SIT), 504 Implementation Team, Multidisciplinary Intervention Team (MDT), or HIB Prevention-Intervention Team. It is also recommended that the targeted student and a member of the targeted student's family be involved in the development of the plan. Once the plan has been developed by the team, the principal or his/her designee will see that it is implemented with the student and his/her family. The principal will also share this plan with all necessary school staff. The classroom teachers will leave a copy of the plan for any **substitute teachers** who come in.

The plan involves two components: the actions **school staff** will engage in and the actions the **student** will engage in. The plan has a **definite start and a proposed end date.** It is meant to cover the **entire school day,** from the time a student boards a bus in the morning until he/she departs the bus at the end of the day. The targeted student needs to be safe during **before-school and after-school activities,** and protected from any **new bullying done by others** in support of the initial aggressor or in retaliation for reporting or discipline actions.

The plan designates a **Primary Staff Contact** for the targeted student. This person might be the staff person to whom the student first reported the HIB, or with whom the student feels most comfortable. It might also be his/her homeroom teacher, counselor or another classroom teacher.

It is the intent of this plan that it be carried out in a way which is **minimally intrusive**. School layout, passing times, grade levels and configurations and availability of staff may impact the plan. It will be necessary to adapted to the building. For example, if there are locations which are known to be particularly dangerous for the student, those areas need to be identified and monitored. (An additional template is available which more closely fit the needs of primary grades.)

HIB - Targeted Student Safety Plan

Student's Name:_____

Primary Staff Contact: _____

Classroom/Homeroom Teacher: _____
Grade Level: _____ Room Number:_____

Plan start date: _____ Proposed End date: _____

A. School/Staff:

1. ❑All school staff will be apprised of this safety plan and will make every effort to implement it successfully.

2. ❑Any school staff who witness or are otherwise made aware of any harassing, intimidating or bullying behavior directed toward the student will intervene immediately and will report such behavior to the principal.

3. Classroom and Passing Times:

    ❑Mr./Mrs. _____ will be designated as the student's primary point of contact (trusted adult) on staff.

    ❑Mr./Mrs. _____, the classroom teacher, will keep the student and his/her aggressor separated in the classroom and during class activities.

    ❑Classroom teachers will keep the student and his/her aggressor separated in the classroom and during class activities

    ❑Our school security officer (or other appropriate staff member) will be visible in the hall and will monitor the student during all passing times.

☐Mr./Mrs. _____ is designated as the student's recess monitor and will be visible and available during recess.

4. ☐The student will visit our school counselor (nurse / principal / AP) on a daily basis at an agreed upon time to ensure that the plan is working. If the student does not or cannot visit this person at that time, the designated person will locate and check with the student.

If you select other, please describe: _____

Why do you think the harassment, intimidation or bullying occurred? _____

_____

Were there any witnesses? Yes ☐No ☐ If yes, please provide their names: _____

_____

Did a physical injury result from this incident? If yes, please describe. _____

_____

Was the target absent from school as a result of the incident? Yes ☐ No ☐ If yes, please describe.

_____

_____

Is there any additional information? _____

_____

Thank you for reporting!

For Office Use

Received by: _____

Date received: _____

Action taken: _____

_____

Parent/guardian contacted: _____

Circle one: Resolved   Unresolved

Referred to: _____

2. Parents are welcome to contact the school at any time to check on the effectiveness of the plan.

If threats and harassment continue and/or escalate, law enforcement may be called in.

This plan is in place from _____ through _____,
at which time it will be reviewed, revised or continued, if necessary.

We agree to the Safety Plan as stated above.

_____	_____
Student	Parent
_____	_____
Principal	Date

Completed / Modified / Extended: _____ (Date)

(http://www.k12.wa.us/SafetyCenter/BullyingHarassment/pubdocs/SampleHIBTargetedStudentSafetyPlan-Primary.doc).

These types of policies, reporting and response procedures stemming from state law form the basis for building safe, bully-free schools. But, developing policies and procedures are only the first step and alone simply are not adequate for the kinds of moral transformation necessary to stem bullying activity. Next, districts and schools must develop programs focused on all stakeholders and constituencies. As outlined in Chapter 2, there are a number of pre-packaged programs on the market, but often these can be quite expensive. Common to most anti-bullying, school-based programs are the following elements:

AT THE SCHOOL LEVEL:[3]

- Student surveys—this is aimed a better understanding the prevalence of bullying within the school and, perhaps, the forms that it takes. The Olweus program provides a questionnaire to accomplish this task.
- Increased student monitoring—this is aimed at both assessment ('noticing' how much and what kind of bullying activity takes place in the school) as well as enforcement (looking for bullying activity and responding appropriately).
- Involvement of parents—this is aimed at parent awareness (via training, conversation, etc.) as well as recruiting parents into the response process (to discipline and monitor their own children who bully and to support and strengthen their own children who are targets of bullying).

AT THE CLASSROOM LEVEL:

- A curriculum teaching tolerance as well as communication, anger management and conflict resolution skills. This often is taught as a unit by the school counselor, but certainly can be led by the classroom teacher and is aimed at student awareness and training.

- Immediate consequences for aggressive behavior and rewards for inclusive behavior. Here, the aim is enforcing policy and bringing change in behavior. The requirement is immediate and consistent response upon discovery.
- Classroom discussion of incidents when they occur. Here, the aim is to create both awareness and a culture surrounding bullying activities. For example, teachers may lead discussion surrounding peer response when they see or know of bullying activities.

AT THE INDIVIDUAL LEVEL:

- Serious personal discussion with bully and victim, and their families. Here, in response to a bullying incident, the individuals involved are reprimanded/taught (bullying), supported/taught (victim) and made aware (parents, students) of the bullying activities, school policies, and consequences.
- Focused assistance to develop alternative behaviors by both. Here, specific training and/or support is put in place in response to the bullying incident. This may include planning or developing individual strategies to stop the specific bullying situation.

As noted, the initial outline above is based on the Olweus anti-bullying program. Several other elements are integral to the Olweus program:

- Acknowledge unequivocally that the primary responsibility for stopping bullying lies with educators rather than with parents or students
- Project a clear, unambiguous stand against bullying
- Include both systems-oriented and individual-oriented components
- Set long-term and short-term goals
- Target the entire school population, not just a few problem students
- Make the program a permanent component of the school environment, not a temporary remedial program
- Implement strategies that have a positive effect on students and on the school climate that go beyond the problem of bullying (2001, Olweus)

The Expect Respect anti-bullying program contains similar elements, connecting bullying and anti-harassment threads:

Assumption

- Whole school approach, training all

Program Components

- Classroom Curriculum (12 weekly sessions—focus on bystanders)
- Staff Training (6 hour trainings—follow-up 3 hours)
- Policy Development
- Parent Education (presentations/newsletters)
- Support Services: counseling/advocacy

The Bully Busters anti-bullying program again contains similar elements, with a more detailed training regimen:

Assumptions of the Program

- Changing the Environment is More Powerful than Changing Individuals
- Prevention is Better than Intervention
- Changing the Environment Requires Support and Understanding Among Teachers

Skills for Bullying Prevention

- ABCs—Antecedents (practice that lends itself to bullying behaviors), Behaviors (behaviors which may stem from certain practices), Consequences (what could happen to students as a result of behaviors)—proactive thinking about classroom/playground/school practice
- Understanding the Spheres of Influence (p. 301)
- Rearrange the Environment (transitions, seatings, etc.)
- Establish Clear Classroom Guidelines and Be Consistent
- Use Respectful, Polite, Clear, and Specific Language
- Avoid Public Confrontations
- Teach New Skills
- Use a Solution-Focused Approach to Problems
- Use the Big Questions
  1. What is the problem and what is my goal?
  2. What am I doing?
  3. Is what I am doing helping me achieve my goal?
  4. If not, what can I do differently that will help me to achieve my goal?
  5. Is my new strategy working?

Program Modules

- Module 1: Increasing Awareness of Bullying
- Module 2: Preventing Bullying in Your Classroom
- Module 3: Building Personal Power
- Module 4: Recognizing the Bully

- Module 5: Recognizing the Victim
- Module 6: Recommendations and Interventions for Bullying Behavior
- Module 7: Recommendations and Interventions for Helping Victims
- Module 8: Relaxation and Coping Skills (2004, outlined in Espelage and Swearer)

The Nebraska Department of Education offers the following outline regarding appropriate anti-bullying programs within schools (http://www.education.ne.gov/index.html):

NEBRASKA DEPARTMENT OF EDUCATION SCHOOL-WIDE PREVENTION AND INTERVENTION

The most effective anti-bullying plan is designed and implemented with specific knowledge and skills consistently trained and used throughout the school district. This plan declares a school's commitment to creating a safe, caring and respectful learning environment for all students. A bullying prevention and intervention plan adopted by the district might include specific behavior programs, forms used, philosophies of interactions, curriculum, or basic protocols. Effective anti-bullying programs or curriculum implement a scope and sequence of knowledge and skills to be learned by all students and requires school-wide involvement and support. Students involved in bullying situations benefit from additional instruction specific to their role as one using bullying behaviors, as a target, or as a bystander/witness.

Prevention Strategies

Prevention is best addressed by communicating and teaching the expected pro-social behaviors.

- Clearly communicate policy and protocols for bullying behaviors to all staff, students and parents
- Discussion and presentations about bullying and caring behaviors are ongoing
- Empower bystanders to promote and take responsibility for creating a safe and welcoming environment
- Provide a means for safely reporting bullying behaviors
- Staff are observant and responsive to reports of bullying
- Students are recognized for caring behaviors
- Adopt a social skills curriculum
- Monitor and adjust local bullying prevention program based on analysis of local school data and best practices in the field of bullying prevention (change in supervision, use of resources, methods of communication, reporting procedures, etc.)

Bystander/Witness Interventions

Activating and empowering the bystanders/witnesses through education about bullying and practice (role plays) in intervening is the most impactful intervention. Group training for bystanders includes emphasizing that there is strength in numbers and that permission is given with the expectation to intervene respectfully and safely or report the bullying behaviors. Determining specific bystander interventions depends on analyzing the level of risk of a particular bullying situation.

School/Classroom Strategies for Bystanders

- Talk about it with the class
- Emphasize strength in numbers
- Explain the expectation to take action
- Teach and practice skills and strategies to take a stand
- Empower witnesses to take leadership roles in making the school safe for everyone
- Acknowledge and reinforce caring behaviors
- Clarify the difference between tattling and telling (reporting).

Individual Strategies for Bystanders

- Make a safe choice; consider the level of risk in choosing an action for intervening.
- Teach options for intervening:
    - Choose to not participate
    - Report to an adult
    - Encourage the peer group to take a stand
    - Take an individual stand
    - Be friendly toward the target

Target Interventions

Targets need to be supported by a third party and have their reports taken seriously. Target interventions typically include teaching social skills such as friendship, assertiveness and anger management skills. Interventions for targets may be done one-on-one or in a support group. Targets should not be re-victimized by bringing the target and perpetrator together to try to resolve the situation.

School/Classroom Strategies for Targets

- Provide a safe place to report; take all reports seriously

Toward a Holistic Anti-Bullying Model 129

- Assign new or needy students to a buddy
- Assign a caring staff member to "connect" regularly with the students who are potential targets
- Get a caring majority in the classroom; use class meetings/discussion to teach expected behaviors and model value of each person
- Consider how students are grouped so that the targets are not left out and are not paired with someone who bullies them.
- Teach friendship and assertiveness skills.

Individual Strategies for Targets

- Provide options for preventing bullying incidents
  - Avoid the bully
  - Stay in safe areas
  - Share your feelings with someone you trust

- Provide options for responding to bullying incidents
  - Walk away
  - Make an assertive statement, then walk away
  - Tell an adult

Bullying Behavior Interventions

School discipline policies, while needed to address student conduct issues and support positive student behaviors, are not sufficient to address bullying behaviors. Bullying behavior interventions may include teaching social skills such as friendship, empathy and anger management in one-on-one settings, not in a group setting. Discipline should be addressed privately. Interventions focus on identifying the expected behaviors.

School/Classroom Strategies for Bullying Behaviors/Perpetrators of Bullying

- Equalize the power—work one on one
- Challenge distorted thinking.
- Use consistent, predictable discipline
- Focus on behaviors and expectations
- Use a problem-solving approach
- Forward documentation to a central location to be reviewed regularly

Individual Strategies for Bullying Behaviors/Perpetrators of Bullying

- State (do not ask) rule violated, feelings of target, and plan of action

- Teach social skills
  - Friendship skills
  - Empathy skills
  - Emotional self awareness
  - Social awareness
- Develop personal management skills
  - Anger and emotion management
  - Assuming personal responsibility
- Provide pro-social consequences (2012 Nebraska Department of Education)

The typical anti-bullying programs, containing elements similar to those listed above, focus on four main responses to bullying activity:

1. Assessment—determining what level of bullying behavior is active within the school.
2. Response to active bullying (bully—reprimand, rules, incentives, training; victim—support, training)
3. Monitoring—adult surveillance targeted on typical high-risk areas (passing periods, playground, cafeteria, etc.).
4. Informational/Training campaigns (students, staff, parents)—poster campaigns, assemblies, classroom sessions, etc.

While certainly these programs have nuanced approaches, they also contain similar responses to bullying activities within schools. Research shows that such programs can be effective, but the degree of effectiveness is at best uneven. Yet, these kinds of responses are, again, a minimum starting point (policies, procedures, programs, training) if we are to work toward issues of safety on the school campus when it comes to bullying, intimidation and harassment. These types of systems must become a regular aspect of school practice.

But, as I have argued, these steps (assessment, monitoring, reprimand and reward), while necessary, often work to address the typical understandings of bullying motivation (lack of information, skill deficiency, school culture that overtly encourages bullying, etc.) and the more common conception of moral education (rational instruction, reprimand, reward, and surveillance). And, as I have laid out in previous chapters, such responses often fall flat because they often don't take into account the 'I like' of bullying activity (the satisfaction of bullying) or the stories which direct 'need meeting' in schools. I now turn to a transformative response that aims to stop bullying activity before it stops.

RESPONSE AND TRANSFORMATION

It is a given that my discussion in the above section (Response and Safety) outlines the foundational elements that all schools must have in place to work towards creating safe learning environments for all students in relation to bullying. In turning to more 'transformative' responses, I do not see this section as a replacement to the previous section, but instead, but instead as an addition to the policy, procedure and training responses outlined above. But, my research-based assumption is that the complexity of bullying activity calls for more than informational training, skill development and monitoring by adults. We must wade into the world of transformative, moral education as it relates to bullying activities in schools if we are to see consistent and lasting change. Here I focus on three broad elements: Identity and Need, Story and School Culture, and Tools of Transformation.

Identity—Meeting Foundational Needs

If, as I have suggested, public bullying activity (and, remember, 85% of all bullying activity is done in a public setting in view of on-looking peers) is situated in an attempt to gain status in the eyes of peers and, if status, is integral to identity construction (i.e., we develop a sense of self from others), then paying attention to the processes of identity construction within schools becomes important to our anti-bullying efforts. I have argued that bullying behavior, like most behavior, is need-based. In other words, Jake's desire to 'be someone' in the eyes of his peers in the bump game moved him to humiliate Matthew in front of them. And, when they smiled and high-fived him the tears of Matthew became satisfying to a certain degree (this helps us pay attention to Jake's 'I like'). Here, bullying activity involves an exchange (Jake received something in the humiliation of Matthew). That exchange, if we can articulate it, is key to understanding both the motivation and the pathways of bullying activity. One of the ways we can circumvent the need to 'be someone' through the public humiliation of a peer is to work toward meeting that need (e.g., to be someone) in our students in other ways. If we can do so, we might circumvent the 'desire' to bully to 'be someone' because that need is already being met in more humane ways. In addition, Jake's attempt to create a sense of identity through dominance, as I have argued, will always fall flat because a sense of self can only be established through reciprocal relationships, not through the one-way relations of humiliation. Thus, even in Jake's attempt to create a sense of identity through dominance, the need to build a healthy identity will elude him. What, then, can we do in schools to foster a healthy sense of identity within our students? Here I offer two suggestions.

First, we need to provide monitored and supported encounters between students, teachers and staff as an integral aspect of schooling itself. Schooling is primarily focused on academic achievement, even more so in the current culture of high stakes testing and academic standardization. We certainly don't put schools on probation because the level of friendship within the building isn't high enough. But, we do indeed do so if academic achievement lags. While student relationships with other students and with teachers are important components of interest within schooling, typically even this interest is directed toward academic achievement. Recess becomes a place for students to expend energy and for teachers and students to "take a break" *in order* to stay productive and focused in the classroom. Passing periods are simply that (no dawdling!). They offer the minimum amount of time for students to pass to their next class. Lunch, thoroughly supervised, is a place to "fuel up," helping students to have the energy to stay academically focused in class. This is not to argue that within schooling such relational spheres are not seen as important times of interaction; spaces where students can learn to get along and form democratic relational skills (e.g., sharing, cooperative game playing, self-control, etc.). Here I simply argue that in shear time allotment and often in focus these "relational spaces" pale in light of academic concerns. Further, many schools do attend to "teaching" the rubrics of relationships. Placards on respect, assemblies on bullying or teasing, class discussions of relational norms, etc. are all a part of school culture. But, if 'selves' are only constructed in the actual encounter with another, teaching about respect and rushed passing periods will miss the mark (Jacobson 2007b, 191)

Here, then, creating structures such as school-wide small groups, advisory periods, and small schools approaches become helpful. Schools may decide to create regular small group encounters, perhaps including all humans within the building (e.g., groups made up of staff, students, and faculty from diverse perspectives and position) where the main goal is connection. Advisory periods could be used to direct healthy conversation, reflection, and interaction. The main impetus behind the small schools approach (e.g., breaking a larger comprehensive school in smaller 'sub-schools' within the same building) is aimed at a more personal, connected school experience. These are not new ideas, but the point here is not only to change the structure, but to facilitate reciprocal relationship. As we know, simply putting students in small learning groups does not mean that they will function well and that learning will take place. Instead, we must manage those groups (in terms of membership, content, roles, and the atmosphere of participation). If the goal is healthy reciprocal relationship, then we must train facilitators to foster such relationship, we must manage the groupings of students/humans toward such ends, and we must constantly reflect and evaluate so that the functionality of such groups stays effective and focused. I am convinced that schools can accomplish this task without a huge investment of time or money, but not without a deep transformation in their philosophies of education. Relationship must become as important as academics. The same attention we give to data-driven assessment, to classroom management, and to differentiated instruction, we must also give to healthy student interaction, to the recognition of each human in the school, and to connection. If these needs are at the heart of bullying, then meeting these needs in the day-to-day interactions that our students have will lessen the need to find significance through domination. If you've just had dinner, you're less likely to steal a loaf of bread because you're hungry. Hence, if one already 'has a place to stand' in the school with peers, then the need to carve out such a space by humiliating a classmate becomes less attractive.

In terms of identity, a second strategy seems important. While I will address this more fully in my next sub-point on school culture, it is connected here specifically to 'education' surrounding issues of identity. Of course, embedded in any middle school curricula are conversations around identity construction (who do I want to be? What do others think of me?), among other important transition conversations regarding body changes, responsibility, health, sound judgments, etc. My argument is that identity processes are involved in all stages of human existence, especially so for children and, thus, should be part of our conversations within schools. Students already have a sense of who 'counts' within the schools and who doesn't. They've learned that from parents, from peers, from the media, from teachers, etc. I argue, here, that we should join this conversation in intentional ways across the learning spectrum. Hence, if bullying is situated in identity construction, then raising and problematizing the subjects or topics at play in such productions may raise fresh questions for students to consider, offering new horizons from which to understand the ourselves in light of others. Here, within the curricula of schooling, I propose that we begin to discuss with our students a range of topics that seem to be connected to bullying activities. These topics, stemming from my earlier discussions are not limited to, but would include topics such as status, dominance, identity, legitimacy, inclusion, personal value, the preferred self, motivation through comparison, strengths and weaknesses not as status symbols, but as markers of what we 'bring to the table', achievement, who counts (in the school, at home, in the marketplace) and why, etc. If bullying is one answer to the question of "status," then our work is to not only teach students not to bully, or even to teach what 'good' status is, but to problematize status itself, allowing students to be put at risk (e.g., *Oh, status is not what I thought it was*). Included in these "subjects of the self" would be (in Benjaminian fashion) discussions regarding subject/object relations, tensions between assertion and being asserted upon, as well as (in Foucauldian fashion) discussions surrounding subjectivity narration, systems and discourses of narration, value in schooling, motivation within schooling, etc. Here, I suggest a curriculum of discussion centered upon the subjects which I have argued are at play in bullying activities and identity construction.[4] These discussions may be weekly events or a daily part of classroom discourse, but should not be rhetorical discussion (where the teacher seeks to "teach" students through raising specific questions looking for specific answers). The aim here is to begin honest questioning surrounding important subjects, perhaps allowing the space, as new horizons of understanding to develop around crucial topics, for self-knowledge and growth. Notice, throughout this section I have repeatedly used the word 'discussion.' Thinking back to the chapters outlining moral education, it is precisely in this kind of

134 *Rethinking School Bullying*

work that we must consider Dewey's notion of 'direct conveyance' and it's ineffectiveness, Lakatos' auxiliary band, and Paley's strategy for shifting disposition. Simply teaching these topics (i.e., via direct conveyance), will fall flat according to Dewey, Lakatos, and Paley. In fact, many of our current anti-bullying programs do just this. For example, if we want students to respect each other, we give them information on respect, we model it for them (again, typically in an instructional vein), we put up placards around the school with respect mottos, and we watch students to reprimand and reward=. When we do this we treat bullying as primarily a rational issue, often disregarding the ways that disposition is formed and transformed. In contrast, in these conversations we are not targeting the direct core belief (e.g., bullying is a good way to status), but instead focus on the auxiliary band surrounding and protecting that belief (e.g., status, who counts, why being on top seems to give more status, etc.). By attacking the auxiliary belief, working continuously over a long period of time, we have a stronger possibility of impacting the core belief in an indirect fashion. This does not mean that we should never teach or directly discuss bullying; but, if Lakatos' research is correct, the heart change we want will only come as we target the auxiliary band in a concerted fashion.

Here, again, Dewey argues that it is the experience/culture that we create surrounding a moral dilemma that begins to shift our dispositions. Again, this can involve teaching, but mainly it must involve non-direct conveyance that allows like-mindedness to occur. Paley offers a prime example of this. She discusses the new rule she'd like to institute (i.e., 'you can't say you can't play) with her students and with others over the course of several months. In open-ended conversation, pushing thinking, but often not giving the definitive answer, she allows her students to voice their concerns, to surface their passions, and, eventually, to begin to buy in to her new rule. This is the kind of conversation that will be necessary to fundamentally shift how our students view status and how it is gained within the school. But, of course, we are beginning to imagine here the shifting of culture. This leads into a second major focus for a holistic, transformative anti-bulling approach.

A New Story—Guiding Pathways

Of course, in these conversations we are beginning to re-imagine hierarchy and how it plays out in school culture. As discussed in Chapter 5, the current culture of schooling motivates students by comparison and, thus, instills systems of hierarchy. Being the captain of the football team brings with it certain recognition and status. Being a mediocre football player brings less. It would be unthinkable in current school culture to honor the 'worst' student in the school, but would make complete sense to award a prize to the top students (a prize that would typically be presented at an assembly with hundreds of on-looking peers and adults).

Again, comparison is not necessarily a bad thing and motivating students to excel is certainly admirable. But, most students in such a culture walk around as an ordinary person in a "Princess Diana" world. In other words, only a few can be top students, athletes, school news reporters, etc. The others simply fade into the periphery. But, here's the rub; the culture of schooling clearly indicates that the best, the top, in other words the ones who dominate, are recognized. The rest are not. In such a system, bullying begins to make sense. As I stated earlier, one way to view Jake's bullying of Matthew is to conclude that he simply took the rhetoric of school more seriously than his peers. Telling him to stop is not only like telling a man dying of thirst not to drink the glass of water in front of him, it requires the thirsty man to ignore the 'normal' pathways for meeting that need during the day (e.g., stopping by the drinking fountain, bringing something to drink from home, buying a bottle of water in the cafeteria). We may work to meet the needs at the heart of bullying, as we discussed in the previous section (concrete relational interaction), but we must also adjust the pathways of need-meeting (status through dominance, or status through some other avenue) available within the cultures of schooling. Though I've intimated that school culture in monolithic, each school and district is different and, thus, imbibes its own nuanced rhetoric of value. That's why, I argue, our current anti-bullying programs work in some school and not others. Given certain cultures, they match up in ways that motivates students. Given other cultures, they are not powerful enough to combat what is already in place.

As we discussed in Chapter 6, culture is often invisible (we swim in the water without much reflection regarding what kind of water it is) and, yet, is always constructed. Here we have two tasks. First, we need to unearth the kind of culture that operates in the specific settings in which students find themselves. This could be in the home (for parents), this could be in youth organizations (for youth workers), but here we will focus on schools (for teachers and administrators). The primary way we unearth the kind of 'water' that we swim in is through reflective questioning. This process should involve a range of stakeholders (which I will touch on shortly), but will certainly involve concerted questioning of the course of a year or two. What kinds of questions might we ask? The questions should focus not only on ferreting out the culture already in operation, but also on the desired culture. Figure 8.1 provides a suggested list.

General Questions

- What are the strengths of our school? (Why is it good to be a teacher, a staff person, a student, or a parent/family member associated with our school?)
- What, overall, do we hope our school will be known as? (What are some salient characteristics that describe our school?)

- What is your experience with school bullying?
- Why is stopping bullying activity important at our school? (Why does it matter to you personally, in your role within the school, to our educational aims, and to student well-being?)
- Where have I seen/been aware of bullying within our school in the last year?
- When you think of "moral education," what is your reaction? (interests, fears or concerns, etc.)
- In terms of your own moral compass (i.e., what you think is right or wrong, how you monitor and control your own behavior, etc.), where did that come from and how did it get instilled?
- If "character education" (per No Child Left Behind) were to be a fundamental aspect of the work of our school, and your own work in the classroom, what might that entail?

Institutional Questions

- What is the "cultural story" of our school?
  - Who counts and who doesn't and why? (staff, students, families)
  - Who knows each other and who doesn't and why? (staff, students, families)
  - Who leads and who doesn't and why? (staff, students, families)
  - What matters in our school and what doesn't and why?
- How open or resistant is our school to real change? Why do you think that? How does change get enacted in our school?
- Where are the main educational resources of our school allocated?
  - What professional development programs are brought in and who makes those decisions?
  - What assembly/special programs are brought in and who makes those decisions?
- What is the social climate of our school? (Do all get along? Are there cliques? Are there hierarchies? If so, who's in each and why? Is it cross-disciplinary/cross-grade level?)
  - How would you describe collegiality among the teaching faculty here? (i.e., do you collaborate with other teachers, do you feel "connected" to other teachers here, are there regular discussions/collaborations around various topics among teachers?)
  - How would you describe the collegiality between administration and faculty at our school?
  - How would you describe the partnership between parents/families and staff at our school?
- Generally, what are people striving for here?
- Do most students feel like they belong here? What makes you think that?

- Are there outsiders here (staff, students, or parents)? What makes them outsiders?
- How is difference tolerated at our school? (by staff, students, and parents)

Aims (vision-casting)

- Regarding bullying, what are our aims as a school on a general level (what kind of school do we hope to be) as well as a specific level (what kinds of activities, mindsets, social interactions, vision do we hope our school will reflect?)
- What is your vision about who should count or be valued at our school and what that "value" should be based upon?
- What is your vision for "relational connections" at our school? What do you hope for in student-student, student-teacher, teacher-teacher, teacher-staff/administration relationships?
- What is your vision for identity construction at our school? (the way you, other teachers, administration, families and students come to see themselves as a result of their experience at our school).

Structures (what to put into place)

- In order to alter any "stories" that we aren't happy with (listed in the "Institutional Questions" section), what structures might need work, dismantling, and/or rebuilding?
- To accomplish our aims (listed in the previous section), what new structures might need to be built?
- In our list of old and new "structures," what stories might each tell and not tell?

Leadership (who will lead, monitor, cast vision?)

- Who should lead this effort and why? (in general—staff, students, parents?; specifically—which people or positions?)
- What kinds of leadership will it take to accomplish the above? (aggressive, collaborative, etc.)
- Looking over the list of various "teams" needed in this process, which team would you be most interested in serving on and why?

Action (what actions are next and what is our timeline?)

- What are the first next steps in this process? When will they be taken and by whom?

> - Thinking about an overall time-table to accomplish these aims and re-storying, what might the process look like over the course of the next two years?
> - What responsibilities/tasks will leadership need to take up to help this process stay on track?
> - What responsibilities/tasks will various teams/staff/students/parents need to take up to help this process move along?
> - What responsibilities/tasks will you need to take up in order to help this process along? What's your next step and when will you take it?
>
> **Evaluation (how will we know if we're making progress?)**
>
> - How will we measure success?
> - Who will measure our success?
> - When will we evaluate?
> - What kinds of tools will we need to evaluate?

Figure 8.1 Strategy-building questions.

This list of questions certainly can be expanded or altered, but these are the kinds of reflective questions that help us to understand the cultural aspects the bullying activities swim within and, more importantly, allow us to reimagine a school culture that provides alternative pathways for the needs of bullying to be met. In other words, by altering the culture we provide a pathway of exchange that may not include status through domination. But, remember, moral education (including changing culture—which essentially means transforming what people view as important) does not primarily happen via direct conveyance and there will be resistance (per Lakatos and Paley). Thus, this process of cultural transformation will involve leadership that is willing to pursue this project over the long term and regular, consistent engagement by all stakeholders. This would require regular engagement with students, teachers, staff, administration, parents, community organizations and community members.

In the midst of this process, likely providing a catalyst for this 'culture discussion' it is recommended that the school begin to work on its own anti-bullying strategy. The strategy, again, must move beyond simple campaigns and slogans, to a focus on transformation of the culture of the school as well as of each human being associated with it. Figure 8.2 provides an outline of the possible stakeholders who could provide the structure for ongoing conversation and activity in this culturally transformative anti-bullying process. I have couched the terminology in terms of 'teams' that would meet regularly to discuss around specific themes related to bullying and school culture. It is important that these teams include members from all stakeholder groups (e.g., parents, teachers, administrators, community partners, and students).

- **Policy:** What do we believe here? (Task: What is/should be our policy?)
- **Assessment:** What bullying happens here? (Task: Are students being bullied here and to what extent?)
- **Culture:** What is the culture of our school as it comes to elements surrounding bullying and status here? (Task: Do we motivate via hierarchical comparison? What story do we want to adopt in our school? How might we go about that?)
- **Campaign:** Rules, consequences, culture (Task: How are we/should we communicating policy/culture?)
- **Training:** Assessment, philosophy, culture (Task: How are we/should we be training students, staff and parents?)
- **Intervention:** Student, teacher, parent (Task: What are/should be our intervention points?)
- **Monitoring:** Student, teacher, parent (Task: Are we following through with the above on all levels?)
- **Evaluation:** How are we doing? (Task: How are we doing as a whole? Is bullying activity decreasing, increasing, or staying level as a result of our efforts?)

Figure 8.2 Strategic teams.

I have listed here an example of the kinds of tools that can be used, both to re-envision school culture as well as groupings of individuals to help form, propagate and create buy-in for such a vision. But, I have not explicitly articulated the kind of culture which may undermine the current 'status-through-dominant-comparison' culture which often is used to motivate students in our schools. To touch on this I turn to a likely familiar story, but one that at its core may offer some additional insight.

In September of 2007 a story surfaced via CBC News of two twelfth-graders who decided to intervene in the bullying of a ninth-grade classmate (http://www.cbc.ca/news/canada/story/2007/09/18/pink-tshirts-students.html?ref=rss). The September 18 article, *Bullied Student Tickled Pink by Schoolmates' T-shirt Campaign* (2007), outlines the story of two Nova Scotia students who took a stand. A ninth-grade boy at Central Kings Rural High school wore a pink shirt on the first day of school. He was targeted by classmates who threatened to beat him up. When they became aware of the incident, two upper classmen went to a local store and bought fifty pink shirts. Contacting their friends, the next day they wore their newly purchased shirts to support the freshman student. But, as word got out, hundreds of classmates actually joined in to create a 'sea of pink' in solidarity with their classmate that had been targeted (CBC 2007).

In the article Shepherd discusses two important results from the 'sea of pink': first, the look of relief on the victim's face as he walked into school that morning and, second, the fact that the bullying of this victim had completed ceased as of the print date of the article. This article brings strong confirmation of the research outlined in Chapter 6; that one of the strongest correlates to the avoidance of bullying by a potential victim involves the number and kinds of friendships he or she develops. These friendships provide a social buffer for the victim. Why might this be? First, because the types of friendships we develop allow for acceptability within school circles (i.e., create status for those within a peer clique or crowd). Second, victims are likely targeted because the bully has determined in advance that they will not, or cannot effectively, retaliate. Having friends in high places mitigates the vulnerability of the victim. Hence, a number of anti-bullying programs focus, rightly, on the development of peer support groups. But, for a peer to stand up for a victim means they already have to believe a story that compels them to take the risk involved in standing up to a potentially powerful bully. The question we're wrestling with her is how to foster that cultural story within those peers. Somehow Shepherd and Price were willing and had a desire to stand up for their classmate. The moral education that I've been advocated toward in the past three chapters is aimed at the sort of 'heart' transformation. In essence, Shepherd and Price became the older boys in Mrs. Wilson's back yard.

But, what is the story that is being told here? There are two, among many, storylines that I want to consider from this incident. First, one could conclude that what happened when Shepherd and Price, and the hundreds of other students who wore pink that day, is that the victim's 'difference' was erased. In other words, by a number of students, and of course including those with enough social clout to matter, wearing pink the fact that the victim also wore pink was mainstreamed. In fact, this is the storyline that many anti-bullying programs seek to take up when training the victim to be less 'victimish.' Here, those qualities of the victim that are outliers (e.g., the fact that Matthew cried easily, the fact that she has a lisp, the fact that he wears unusual glasses, etc.). As the thinking goes, if we can train the victim to not exhibit these differences, to help them 'fit in' to the mainstream, then their targetability will disappear. But, this mainstreaming of students, I argue, is problematic on a two levels. First, many of these differences ultimately are difficult, if not impossible, to 'fix.' The social awkwardness of a ninth-grader isn't remedied in a meaningful way through a number of training sessions. Lisps, bad eye site, body type, etc. are often inherited, not created. And, more importantly, we must ask an essential question here: In our efforts to eradicate bullying by making mainstreaming a victim, what do we lose in the process? Do we want to take away the sensitivity of Matthew, molding a future in which men don't show emotion because it's currently culturally suspect within schooling? I'm not sure we want to build a world full of assertive, non-emotional men just to avoid the possibility of bullying. In fact, I'm not convinced that Matthew's tears or the fact that the victim in the Nova Scotia story wore a pink shirt is actually at the heart of the problem. As I mentioned earlier, for the right students such choices make them trendsetters, not outliers. This, precisely, leads to a second storyline we might draw from the pink shirt encounter.

Could it be that what happened culturally in this Canadian high school is that the victim went from outlier to trendsetter? Rather than Shepherd and Price trying to erase the difference between them and the victim, they actually decided to allow the victim to have a voice, to lead. Here, the victim was given value in the school culture. And, in that valuing of difference, he wasn't erased; instead, he was allowed to speak (or, more importantly, he was listened to).

Harkening back to Foucault, we have moved from motivating by valuing some and allowing others to compare how they stack up, to valuing all, allowing difference to become a foundational element in schooling. While the story of 'difference' is certainly integral to both public and private P-12 schooling (i.e., it is a storyline we profess), the culture of academics truncates its effectiveness. Remember, if every student would receive an "A" automatically, we would likely see two results: (1) Students not trying (because, after all, the differentiating of grades matter) and, (2) Parents of strong students would be upset (because, after all, the differentiating of grades matter to college admissions). Again, this is not to say that moving to a non-graded school house is needed (I actually don't believe this will solve the problem of bullying!). But, it is to say that the differentiation within schooling, the creation of hierarchical comparison is a major tool in how we motivate students to excel. And, as I have argued, in such a system, when value becomes linked to comparison, bullying becomes a natural way of meeting the need for status. Here, we need to shift the story of value.

Instead of "race to the top" we might choose a different slogan: "what do you bring?" Trying to avoid sounding cliché, every student brings something to the school and to society; and, the fact that each brings something different is what makes it work. Setting an academic bar is not problematic in and of itself, but expecting all to be exemplary in math, or science, or writing, or sports, or speech, etc., valuing those who are 'the best' (and, thus, calling the others to try harder) is inconsistent with the difference that we all bring. The truth is, some students have incredible gifts in mathematics, while others show promise in science, while still others excel in the arts. Expecting all to be exemplary in every subject simply is not reasonable. In addition, expecting all to 'reach the top' in some generic bar (get a full ride scholarship to Berklee School of Music, be the new Google superstar programmer), negates the more ordinary, and yet necessary and extraordinary contributions that each human can quietly make. The story becomes not 'how do you measure up?', but 'what do you bring to the table?' Here, we push students to use what they have, honing those talents and abilities for their own sake, valuing what they bring whether it measures up to their neighbor or not. Thus, we move motivation from 'how do you stack up?' to a more individualistic view of striving to pay attention to who are students are and creating dispositions to excel. This does not mean that we shouldn't push all students toward proficiency in math, but we motivate differently. For example, we teach parents not to motivate by saying, "what can't you be more like your sister?" Yet, this is exactly the rhetoric we employ in schools. In parenting we instead value our children, seeking to understand who they are and what they bring, valuing those unique aspects, working to help our children work hard and excel in those and other ways, regardless of how they compare to their siblings. Our students bring an amazing array of talents, abilities and ways of looking at the world. We don't need them to compete for the same prize, we need them to follow a path of growth and expertise based not on how they compare with others, but on where they start, who they are, and level of effort. We value each student's contribution, pushing them hard to grow and excel, but teaching them that sameness isn't the goal; instead, the goal is to bring their unique contributions to the table, contributions that are ultimately needed by schools and societies. This is the kind of narrative that begins to undermine the 'status through dominance' base which underlies bullying. This is the kind of narrative that allowed pink shirts to be a statement of value rather than a means of erasing difference. This is the kind of narrative that gives status to students for their unique contributions, rather than how much better they are than their peers.[5]

Wrapping Up—Tools of Transformation— Change and Moral Identity

In conclusion, allow me to summarize, to raise a helpful notion from Robert Coles, then to bring us back to where we started: Jake and Matthew. In this book I have primarily argued three important points. First, bullying is about attempted status acquisition with peers through public domination. Foundationally bullying is about identity construction, attempting to win the esteem of peers through humiliating a scapegoat in front of those peers. If it didn't work, it would stop. For example, if one could gain status through walking around the school crying or by inserting a dinner plate in their lips students would do it. Why don't they? Because such activities aimed at gaining status don't make sense in the current culture of schooling in the West. Thus, second, bullying continues to flourish in schools (remember, over 80% of all students indicate that they were bullied at some point during their P-12 schooling) because the 'status-through-dominance' mirrors the current story of schooling. Students are motivated to 'race to the top', not to fall to the bottom; and the way they measure their progress is through comparison with their peers. Dominance equals status in schools. We, of course, use other words (those who excel, superstars, the best, the fastest, the strongest, etc.). But, in school those at the head of the class are valued and the rest fight for respect in the trenches. And, finally, in the kinds of moral education we are considering her, we must focus on transforming hearts. Creating students who follow rules only when they are being watched is problematic to eradicating bullying. In fact, bullying prevention programs that don't focus on heart transformation often simply train bullies to be better bullies. While there are rational aspects to moral education, the kind of transformation necessary to cease often deeply-engrained bullying activity will require more than strong talks and colorful posters. A cultural transformation will be required; one that takes seriously the needs that the bully is seeking to satisfy in her activities, the pathways that direct those need-meeting processes, and the stories that shape both understandings and behaviors.

In light of this I have suggested five specific responses:

1. Safety—In line with current anti-bullying research and programs, we must establish laws, policies, procedures, training, and prevention programs. This is our baseline response.
2. Identity Construction—We must pay attention to the ways students create identity within schools (i.e., the pathways available to 'become someone') and, to facilitate such processes, we must provide opportunities for guided and supportive work in fostering healthy face-to-face student relationships, as well as discussion surrounding identity with faculty and students. This must become an integral and equal component of our P-12 educational project.
3. Status and the Auxiliary Band—We must work to elucidate the 'auxiliary band' of beliefs (e.g., status comes through dominance, people think I'm cool when I bully, the person on top is the one that matters, etc.) that surround bullying activity and focus our anti-bullying efforts there. This auxiliary band is much more vulnerable than the hard core of bullying, and thus provides a more viable approach to eradicating the behavior.
4. Story and Internalization—Moral education involves slogans such as 'just say no', but slogans alone won't cut it. As Krathwohl et al. suggest, moral education that is transformative must be internalized. Such internalization, as seen in Dewey and Paley, comes through the buy-in that happens over a long period of time, through intentional conversation, allowing questions to be asked, not always being able to offer neat, clear answers.
5. Re-Storying a School—Finally, to significantly reduce bullying within schools, we must do two things: (1) Dismantle the pathway to status that is connected to dominance and, (2) Construct a new cultural story that allows status to be gained in new ways. But, story is just story unless everyone buys in; meaning, re-storying means involves all stakeholders in meaningful conversations, elucidating current cultural stories, dreaming of alternative stories, and working to tell the new story in every way for weeks and years to come. This process leans heavily on questioning and discussing.

In many ways, the ideas I've shared here, and certainly those that I've advocated for in the current chapter, are not new. Dewey, Plato, Foucault, Freire and an untold host of others have argued for a more nuanced, holistic view of education. And, in fact, pieces of these kinds of aims within schooling do show up in various forms. For example, we do care about student relationships, we do care about the process of learning as well as the object of learning, etc. The notion that moral education is important within schooling and that such education is aimed at 'heart transformation' has been with us from the time of Plato. But, in another way, what I am advocating for, is fundamentally new. I have raised an alternative picture of the 'exchange' involved in bullying, and have brought into relief topics such as the purposes of education, the means for human motivation, and the processes of moral transformation within school settings. What I am calling for, ultimately, is a new meta-narrative of the human condition.

Robert Coles in his work *The Secular Mind* (1999) raises an interesting perspective that seems germane to the larger implications from our discussion. Coles couches his comments in Judeo-Christian story, but it is the deeper meta-narrative that I am interested in here. Coles muses:

> In the biblical chapters that follow the expulsion of Adam and Eve from the Lord's terrain, so to speak, much is made of the consequent and subsequent physical hardship, pain: floods and pestilence and drought; the hunger and illness that accompanied them. But there was, too, the subjectivity that this new life brought: human beings as exiles, as wanderers, as people paying (forever, it seemed) a price for an act of disobedience, a severe transgression that carried with it the death penalty. That inner state was, right off, marked by self-preoccupation—another first, that of a necessary narcissism as a requirement for a creature suddenly at the mercy of the elements, and with a fixed span of time available.
>
> True, after the Flood, the Lord (in Exodus) relents a bit, promises not to be persecutory in the extreme—hence the survival of humankind. But death is our fate, still. We are left to fend for ourselves, and to do so with apprehension either a constant presence or around any corner. But we are also left with a steadily increasing capacity to make the best of our fatefully melancholy situation: the freedom, and need, to explore, to experiment, to master as best we can what we see and touch. (1999, 13)

Even without the religious reference that Coles employs, he outlines an insecure human reality. Here, humans compete for resources, including status, which are both scarce and necessary for existence and thriving. As Pellegrino and Long indicate, bullying is situated in a battle for resources that are in limited supply. In such a world, surrounded by real competitors, humans become both narcissistic and protective. We are "left to fend for ourselves" and we do so with "apprehension either a constant presence or around any corner." Here, Jake didn't have a 'beef' with Matthew. Instead, he was after a resource in short supply; a resource necessary for human survival at Southside K-8. What was that resource? Status; being someone of value in the eyes of the human community that was his world. If bullying (i.e., public dominance of another) was the means to secure that resource, to ask him to stop is like asking a man dying of thirst not to drink the water in front of him. But, to provide status in ways that wouldn't involve the public domination of another (i.e., status that was real and satisfying), would be like providing water for every thirsty person in the school. If, as Coles suggests, our human existence is touched by insecurity, then constructing a world of motivation based on how one stacks up with one's peers consequently will motivate us to dominate. The "I like" of Jake makes sense in such a scenario. The status insecurity he felt, meshed with the 'dominance-driven' motivational story of schooling, led Jake to humiliate Matthew in front of his peers; not because he hated Matthew, but because he wanted to survive and thrive at Southside.

Jake was laughing. The bump crowd was roaring. And Matthew was crying. I have argued that in this mixture of emotion and interaction an exchange was attempted. In the destruction of Matthew, something of substance, seemingly so, was sought. School bullying certainly involves elements of informational misunderstanding, skill deficiency and delinquency. But, what this look at the phenomenon of school bullying has made clear is that school bullying also, perhaps foundationally, involves a search for self, one that becomes insatiable because it denies the very intersubjectivity that such a quest demands. On that Southside playground, as observed by students and teachers alike, we witness a lesson in attempted self-construction following pathways provided by the cultures (i.e., discourses and practices) within which it was embedded.

What is it about the desperation of a third-grader that makes a classmate whisper to another, arranging her demise? What is it about the tears of a sixth-grader that can make a group of peers howl with laughter? These are the questions at the heart this project and foundational to our battle against school bullying. These questions, though, are not only important to our understanding of bullying, but shed light more broadly upon what it means to be human together; i.e., what it means to understand with another, what the desire to dominate might represent and the ways that we are ever so powerfully narrated within the subtleties of everyday life (Jacobson 2007b, 203–204).

Notes

NOTES TO CHAPTER 1

1. This story is a composite of a number of bullying incidents and responses covering a short period of years within one school. Even though the story will read as one seamless event, the actual events were separated by years and at times by players (Matthew transferred after his sixth-grade year, but the bullies continued at his old school). My depiction of school response toward Matthew and his bullies is a meshing of the school response to a variety of bullying situations over that time period.
2. Taylor, Sammy's brother, was two years younger and, thus too young to be on the soccer team. He would just come to watch, but felt the boldness to ridicule a student two years his senior. It is not typical for a fourth grader to bully a sixth grader (which was disconcerting to Matthew). In a sense, one might imagine Taylor simply following Sammy's lead regarding Matthew.

NOTES TO CHAPTER 2

1. I use the concepts of bullying, aggression, and dominance throughout this discussion. In doing so, often employing these terms in close proximity, I do not mean to suggest that they are simply different names for the same phenomena. Succinctly, I define aggression in the classical sense. Aggression, here, simply refers to forceful activities toward another intended to, or having the result of, intimidating or harming another individual. Regarding aggression, Espelage and Swearer argue that "Researchers who study bullying can "borrow" from the aggression literature as they struggle to define and assess bullying behaviors. One well-accepted typology," they continue, "of aggression includes Dodge's (1991) categorization of proactive versus reactive aggression. Proactive or instrumental aggression includes behavior that is directed at a victim to obtain a desired outcome, such as gaining property, power, or affiliation. In contrast, reactive aggression is directed at the victim as a result of an aversive event that elicited anger or frustration on the part of the perpetrator. The majority of bullying has been viewed as proactive aggression because bullies often seek out their targets with little provocation and do so for extended periods of time" (2003, 368). For example, when one student physically hits another or through verbal abuse intends to harm or intimidate another by the use of forceful rhetoric, it may be called aggressive behavior. I use the concept of dominance, again from a similarly classic definition. I define dominance as activities which through intention or consequence subordinate another, thus providing higher status to the

'dominator', typically through the use of power and control. As Long and Pellegrini describe it, "social dominance is a relational variable that orders individuals in a hierarchy according to their access to resources" (2003, 402). For example, when one student seeks to exert power over another in order to establish higher status or to exert control it may be called dominance. Of course, dominance may be established through aggression, but the two terms are not synonymous. In contrast, bullying, as defined by the empirical literature, may not simply be equated with "aggression" or "dominance", but does often employ tactics of aggression or dominance in its activities. I define "bullying" more fully in this chapter.
2. The literature tempers this view, agreeing that tangible external awards may not be sought in bullying, but countering that the reward of status through dominance is often a goal of the bullying interaction.
3. The General Health Questionnaire used in this study, devised by Goldberg and Williams (1991) "contains sub-scales assessing the prevalence of (i) somatic symptoms, e.g. 'felt run down and out of sorts'; (ii) anxiety, e.g. 'felt constantly under strain'; (iii) social dysfunction, e.g. 'felt (un)able to enjoy your normal day-to-day activities'; and (iv) depression, e.g. 'felt that life was entirely hopeless'" (Rigby 2002, 113).
4. This study used the Interpersonal Reactivity Index (IRI) (Davis 1980) to assess empathy levels. The IRI assesses four areas: perspective taking (the ability to adopt the point of view of others); fantasy (transposing oneself into the worlds and feelings of fictitious characters); empathic concern (feeling concern for the misfortune of others), and personal distress (feeling anxious in tense personal situations).
5. In their research focused on dominance and its ties to developmental stages, Pellegrini and Long see dominance as one motivation of the bully, dominance that secures status. "We found that in early phases of group formation in middle school dominance is expressed through bullying and other agonistic strategies. After groups are stabilized and the dominance hierarchy is stabilized, dominance is expressed through more prosocial and cooperative means. In short, bullying is a form of aggression used by individuals to achieve some end, in this case dominance status" (2004, 110).
6. While some research indicates that bullies lack certain social skills and knowledge which, in turn, leads them to aggress, more recent studies suggest that "given that bullying includes indirect forms of aggression, such as lying and spreading rumors that lead to the victim's exclusion from the group, and that physical violence is in most of the cases carefully planned, it is plausible that at least some bullies have a social understanding of their behavior" (Espelage and Swearer 2003, 375). In other words bullies may simply use their social skills toward different ends than non-bullies. In fact, Kaukiainen et al. found that indirect forms of aggression correlated positively with social intelligence (1999, 84).
7. Egan and Perry add that the assertiveness of highly aggressive victims is often ineffectual (1998, 307). It seems, then, that assertiveness can secure one against victimization, but being too assertive may simply invite bullying. A certain balance must be struck requiring certain levels of social awareness and skill.
8. Brown et al.'s research analyzes the permeability of the barriers between crowds, finding that teenagers are able to move more easily between certain crowds ("normals" to "trendies") than others ("normals" to "headbangers") (1994).
9. Eckert (1989) argues that these groupings are also influenced by economic status and family dynamics. For example, a blue-collar family and the typical

economic and relational dynamics that typify its interactions train adolescents to mimic those structures in the forming of crowds with their peers (cited in Brown et al. 1994, 151–152).
10. Rigby, though, tempers this finding with the notion that many victims may not be aware of the larger circle involved in their victimization. In fact, when bullies were asked if they bullied alone or in groups, group bullying seemed to be more prevalent. Again, this may be due to that fact that bullies, rather than taking the blame solely, answered so as to spread their activities to the larger group (2002, 59–60). Here, the research seems to indicate that bullying is both a dyadic and group phenomenon.
11. Such as a small group of friends (e.g., Jake, Sammy, and Jeff) within the larger peer crowd.
12. I consider, here, a number of anti-bullying programs including: Olweus' Bullying Intervention Program (Olweus 1993; Espelage and Swearer 2004); Espelage and Swearer's Ecological Anti-Bullying Approach (2004); Bully Busters (Horne, et al. 2004); Expect Respect (Whitaker, et al. 2004); Bernese Program (Alsaker and Valkanover 2001); A Bullying Intervention Model (Hoover and Oliver 1996); Pika's Common Concern Method (Hoover and Oliver 1996); Rigby's Anti-Bullying Strategy (2002); The No Blame Approach (Maines and Robinson 1992). I use these programs, not because they are the only, most prevalent, or even seen as the most effective anti-bullying approaches in the literature. Instead, I employ these programs because they maintain common elements typical to a wide array of anti-bullying approaches.
13. Succinctly, we see a clear picture of this in Rigby (2002), arguing that schools must articulate clear guidelines, rules, rewards, and consequences to staff, students, and parents (that they might understand). Here several points of understanding become important. Typical elements in a school anti-bullying policy might include:
1. A strong statement of the school's stand against bullying.
2. A succinct definition of bullying.
3. A declaration of the rights of individuals in the school community—students, teachers, other workers and parents—to be free of bullying and (if bullied) to be provided with help and support.
4. A statement of the responsibilities of members of the school community: to abstain personally from bullying others in any way; to actively discourage bullying when it occurs; and to give support to those who are victimized.
5. A general description of what the school will do to deal with incidents of bullying. (For example: the severity and seriousness of the bullying will be assessed and appropriate actions. This may include the use of counseling practices, the imposition of sanctions, interviews with parents, and, in extreme cases, suspension from school.)
6 An undertaking to evaluate the policy in the near and specified future" (2002, 239).
14. One component of the Pika method involves the "bully interview". This interview, based upon information obtained from adult observers of the bullying activity is focused on helping "the bully to understand and believe that the victim's situation is something to be concerned about" (Hoover and Oliver 1996, 61).
15. It is important, here, to note that the actions of the bully, while certainly encompassing individual choice and propensity, is yet depicted by the literature as acting within a social context. For example, Karin Frey argues that in implementing the *Steps to Respect* anti-bullying program that a focus on "environmental contingencies [is] indeed instrumental in reducing playground bullying" (2005, 29). Specifically, Frey argues that the ways peers

view and respond to bullying activities do affect the actions of bullies. Hence, while individual bullies are seen at times as outliers (i.e., delinquents), such positionalities are always mediated by social context. Here, I simply argue that for whatever reasons, the bully is viewed as one who must be rehabilitated or trained, whether through the application of specific peer pressures, reprimand or rewards and consequences.
16. Truly, we are yet in the early days of bullying research—focused research only beginning in the late 1970s or early 1980s. "Most intervention studies," Rigby contends, "of which there have been about a dozen carefully conducted ones, claim not more than a 15% reduction in the incidence of bullying in a school" (2002, 12).

NOTES TO CHAPTER 3

1. Employing these types of anti-bullying responses will be discussed in greater detail in chapter eight.

NOTES TO CHAPTER 4

1. For a deeper consideration of this process, see *A Place to Stand: Intersubjectivity and the Desire to Dominate* (Jacobson 2009a).
2. The research on bullying certainly does implicate family dynamics to propensities toward children becoming bullies or victims, but the complexity of bullying activities certainly precludes us from concluding that family is the decisive factor. Here, I simply use family dynamics to point out the larger disruption of reciprocity that plays into bullying and the ways that such patterns may be established in children.

NOTES TO CHAPTER 5

1. For a broader discussion of Foucault, discipline, and schooling see *Narrating characters: The making of a school bully* (Jacobson 2010a).
2. The defining of delinquency, here, is not directed at rehabilitating the perpetrator, but toward revealing to society the monster they must not become. According to Foucault, it imposed a 'highly specific grid on the common perception of delinquents: to present them as close by, everywhere present and everywhere to be feared' (1995, 286). The defining of delinquency, then "constitutes a means of perpetual surveillance of the population: an apparatus that makes it possible to supervise through the delinquents themselves, the whole social field" (1995, 281). Here, prisons, the Panopticon and the defining and productions of certain forms of delinquency through disciplinary training become aimed toward a surveillance and ordering of society at large (Jacobson 2010a, 279).
3. "Control," write Dreyfus and Rabinow, "must not be applied sporadically or even at regular intervals. Standardization of operation, efficiency, and the reduction of signification necessitate a constant and regular application. . . . To achieve this dream of total docility (and its corresponding increase of power), all dimensions of space, time, and motion must be codified and exercised incessantly" (1983, 154)
4. Recall, here, as discussed in Chapter 4; bullying seems to spike in middle school. Discussing why that might be, Pellegrini and Long argue that: "A

long-standing critique of middle schools and junior high schools, especially in the United States, is that they do not support youngsters' formation of new cooperative, social groups but instead exacerbate fractured social groups by having youngsters attend large schools which simultaneously stress individual *competition, over cooperation"* (Eccles et al., 1998), (Pellegrini and Long 2004, 112, emphasis mine). The argument, here, is that such cultures may actually mix with the developmental and physical changes middle schoolers are experiencing, deepening a propensity to bully.
5. Of course, Foucault argues that this "narration of subjectivity" is often incidental, not the result of the conscious or intentional activities of school leadership. Such narrations become the unintended consequences of the discourses and practices within specific systems.
6. Ken Rigby cites research regarding the incidence of bullying at a Steiner school in England. The Steiner schools specifically work toward creating a non-competitive, non-hierarchical culture within the school. Rivers and Soutter reported that, "unlike other schools where bullying has been assessed, there were no reports of any physical bullying, although there was some teasing and indirect forms of bullying. The overall level of bullying behaviour was unusually low" (cited in Rigby 2002, 205). "The authors," Rigby adds, "suggest on the basis of this study that bullying is a 'situational problem' rather than one that is due to there being bully-prone personalities" (2002, 205). Of course, this is one isolated study and one must be cautious to put too much stock in it, yet it does raise the interesting question—which I also pose—of a possible link between school disciplinary and training discourse—often situated in hierarchy and competition (Othering)—and the similar hierarchical othering of bullying.
7. See *Narrating Characters* (Jacobson, 2010) for a full discussion of Foucault and schooling.
8. Some might conclude that I am dismissing the personal choice and responsibility of the bully here. If she's just a product of her culture, aren't we letting her off the hook for her behavior? There is no question that bullies make a choice to bully. My argument here is not aimed a erasing that responsibility, but instead to highlight the stories that influence our decision-making processes. For a fuller discussion on this, see Jacobson, 2010a.

NOTES TO CHAPTER 6

1. For a further discussion of this dilemma when it comes to morals in public schooling, see *Moral Education and the Academics of Being Human Together* (Jacobson 2010c).

NOTES TO CHAPTER 7

1. As indicated earlier, Simmons contends that girls can walk with arms around each other, seeming to be best friends, while simultaneously bullying one or the other. Unless we actually hear every conversation at every interaction (including eye rolling, almost undetectable shunning, etc.), we cannot police every bullying episode.
2. Lakatos' introduction is actually subtitled: "Science: reason or religion?" (1970, 91).
3. Paley understands that the art of moral transformation involves various aspects; including rules, story, conversation, etc. "I can tell that the children

are pleased as they line up for recess," Paley reflects. "A satisfying balance has been achieved between fact and fiction. Schoolmistress is right: Story is never enough, nor is talk. We must be told, when we are young, what rules to live by. The grownups must tell the children early in life so that myth and morality proclaim the same message while the children are still listening" (1992, 110).

NOTES TO CHAPTER 8

1. See the Florida State Law at: http://www.leg.state.fl.us/Statutes/index.cfm?App_mode=Display_Statute&Search_String=&URL=1000–1099/1006/Sections/1006.147.html.
2. See Swearer, Espelage, and Napolitano (2009), 53–73 for a current listing of legal and policy requirements by state.
3. This list is based on the Olweus Anti-Bullying program (1993).
4. I do not mean, here, that one would raise such terms as "human finitude" or "the preferred Self" with elementary school students. Rather than the technical terms, the key is to create discussions and questions around the notions that they embody. Hence, paying attention to the developmental level of students, we create spaces where questions surrounding these notions can arise.
5. Of course, there are other narratives: Level of effort versus universal goal, process of learning versus end result, etc. (Jacobson, 2007b). The point is not to create 'the' new universal culture of schooling, but instead to help schools to begin to thoughtfully consider culture and motivation, how they link with bullying and moral transformation, then begin the concrete steps of cultural transformation within their buildings. This is possible for every school, but not until schools take seriously the links between current motivational cultures within school and bullying activity.

References

Alsaker, Francoise D., and Valkanover, Stefan (2001). Early Diagnosis and prevention of victimization in kindergarten. In Juvonen, Jaana and Graham, Sandra (Eds.), *Peer harassment in school: The plight of the vulnerable and victimized*. New York: The Guilford Press.

Atlas, Rona S., and Pepler, Debra (1998). Observations of bullying in the classroom. *The Journal of Educational Research, 92*, 86–99.

Baron-Cohen, S., Jolliffe, T., Mortimore, C., and Robertson, M. (1999). Another advanced test of theory of mind: Evidence from very high functioning adults with autism or Asperger Syndrome. *Journal of Child Psychology and Psychiatry and Allied Disciplines, 38*, 813–822.

Benjamin, Jessica (1988). *The bonds of love: Psychoanalysis, feminism, and the problem of domination*. New York: Pantheon Books.

Bjorklund, D.F., and Pellegrini, A.D. (2002). *The origins of human nature: Evolutionary developmental psychology*. Washington DC: American Psychological Association.

Blasi, Augusto (2005). Moral character: A psychological approach. In D.K. Lapsley and F.C. Power (Eds.), *Character psychology and character education* (pp. 67–100). Notre Dame, IN: University of Notre Dame Press.

Bloom, Benjamin S. (1956). *The taxonomy of educational objectives: Handbook I: Cognitive domain*. White Plains, NY: Longman.

Boivin, Michel, Hymel, Shelley, and Hodges, Ernest V.E. (2001). Toward a process view of peer rejection and harassment. In Juvonen, Jaana and Graham, Sandra (Eds.), *Peer harassment in school: The plight of the vulnerable and victimized*. New York: The Guilford Press.

Borg, M.G. (1988). The emotional reactions of school bullies and their victims. *Educational Psychology, 18*, 433–443.

Boulton, Michael J., Trueman, Mark, Chau, Cam, Whitehand, Caroline, and Amatya, Kishori (1999). Concurrent and longitudinal links between friendship and peer victimization: Implications for befriending interventions. *Journal of Adolescence, 22*, 461–466.

Bowers, L., Smith, P.K., and Binney, V. (1994). Perceived family relationships of bullies, victims and bully/victims in middle childhood. *Journal of Social and Personal Relationships, 11*, 215–232.

Brown, Bradford B., Mory, Margaret S., and Kinney, David (1994). Casting adolescent crowds in a relational perspective: Caricature, channel, and context. In Montemayor, Raymond, Adams, Gerald R., and Gullotta, Thomas (Eds.), *Personal relationships during adolescence*. London: Sage Publications.

Brown, D., and Knowles, T. (2007). *What every middle school teacher should know*. Portsmouth, NH: Heinemann.

Brown, Lyn Mikel (2003). *Girlfighting: Betrayal and rejection among girls*. New York: New York University Press.

Chance, M.R.A. (1988). Introduction. In M.R.A Chance (Ed.), *Social fabrics of the mind* (pp. 1–35). Hove, UK: Lawrence Erlbaum Associates.

Coke, J., Batson, C., and McDavis, K. (1978). Empathic mediation of helping: A two-stage model. *Journal of Personality and Social Psychology, 36,* 752–766.

Coles, Robert (1999). The secular mind. Princeton, NJ: Princeton University Press.

Craig, Wendy M., Pepler, Debra, Connolly, Jennifer, and Henderson, Kathryn (2001). Developmental context of peer harassment in early adolescence: The role of puberty and the peer group. In Juvonen, Jaana and Graham, Sandra (Eds.), *Peer harassment in school: The plight of the vulnerable and victimized*. New York: The Guilford Press.

Davis, M.H. (1980). A multidimensional approach to individual differences in empathy. *JSAS Catalog of Selected Documents in Psychology, 10,* 85.

Dewey, John (1944[1916]). *Democracy and education: An introduction to the philosophy of education*. New York: The Free Press.

——— (2000). My pedagogic creed (1897). In Reed, Ronald F. and Johnson, Tony W. (Eds.), *Philosophical Documents in Education*, 2nd edition (pp. 92–100). New York: Addison-Wesley Longman, Inc.

Dodge, K.A. (1991). The structure and function of reactive and proactive aggression. In Pepler, D.J. and Rubin, K.H. (Eds.), *The development and treatment of childhood aggression* (pp. 201–216). Hillsdale, NJ: Lawrence Erlbaum Associates.

Doll, Beth, Song, Samuel, and Siemers, Erin (2004). Classroom ecologies that support or discourage bullying. In Espelage, Dorothy L. and Swearer, Susan M. (Eds.), *Bullying in American schools: A social-ecological perspective on prevention and intervention*. Mahwah, NJ: Lawrence Erlbaum Associates.

Dressel, Paul (1958). *Evaluation in the basic college at Michigan State University*. New York: Harper.

Dreyfus, Hubert L., and Rabinow, Paul (1983). *Michel Foucault: Beyond structuralism and hermeneutics*. Chicago: The University of Chicago Press.

Duncan, Renae D. (2004). The impact of family relationships on school bullies and their victims. In Espelage, Dorothy L. and Swearer, Susan M. (Eds.), *Bullying in American schools: A social-ecological perspective on prevention and intervention*. Mahwah, NJ: Lawrence Erlbaum Associates.

Eccles, J., Wigfield, A., and Schiefele, U. (1998). Motivation to succeed. In N. Eisenberg (Ed), *Handbook of child psychology*, Vol. 3 (1017–1096). New York: Wiley.

Eckert, Penelope (1989). *Jocks and burnouts: Social categories and identity in the high school*. New York: Teachers College, Columbia University.

Egan, Susan K., and Perry, David (1998). Does low self-regard invite victimization? *Developmental Psychology, 34,* 299–309.

Eisenberg, N., and Miller, P.A. (1987). The relation of empathy to prosocial and related behaviors. *Psychological Bulletin, 101,* 91–119.

Endresen, I.M., and Olweus, D. (2001). Self-reported empathy in Norwegian adolescents: Sex differences, age trends, and relationship to bullying. In Bohard, A.C., Arthur, C. and Stipek, D.J. (Eds.), *Constructive and destructive behavior: Implications for family, school, and society* (pp. 147–165). Washington, DC: American Psychological Association.

Eslea, Mike, and Smith, Peter K. (1998). The long-term effectiveness of anti-bullying work in primary schools. *Educational Research, 40,* 2, 203–218.

Espelage, Dorothy L., Mebane, Sarah E., and Adams, Ryan S. (2004). Empathy, caring, and bullying: Toward an understanding of complex associations.

In Espelage, Dorothy L., and Swearer, Susan M. (Eds.), *Bullying in American schools: A social-ecological perspective on prevention and intervention*. Mahwah, NJ: Lawrence Erlbaum Associates.
Espelage, Dorothy L., and Swearer, Susan M. (2003). Research on school bullying and victimization: What have we learned and where do we go from here? *School Psychology Review, 32*, 365–383.
(Eds.) (2004). *Bullying in American schools: A social-ecological perspective on prevention and intervention*. Mahwah, NJ: Lawrence Erlbaum Associates, Publishers.
Fabre-Cornali, D., Emin, J.C., and Pain, J. (1999). Pupil and parent attitudes towards bullying in primary schools. *European Journal of Psychology in Education, 25*, 207–219.
Farley, R.L. (1999). *Does a relationship exist between social perception, social intelligence and empathy for students with a tendency to be a bully, victim or bully/victim?* Honours Thesis. Adelaide: Psychology Department, University of Adelaide.
Feshbach, N.D. (1997). Empathy: The formative years. Implications for clinical practice. In Bohart, A.C. and Greenberg, L.S. (Eds.), *Empathy reconsidered: Directions for psychotherapy* (pp. 33–59). Washington, DC: American Psychological Association.
Foucault, Michel (1995 [1977]). *Discipline & punish: The birth of the prison*. New York: Vintage Books.
Frey, C., and Hoppe-Graff, S. (1994). Serious and playful aggression in Brazilian girls and boys. *Sex Roles, 30*, 249–269.
Frey, Karin S. (2005). *Observed reductions in bullying, victimization, and bystander encouragement: Longitudinal evaluation of a school-based intervention*. Unpublished manuscript.
Furlong, Michael J., Morrison, Gale M., and Greif, Jennifer L. (2003). Reaching an American consensus: Reactions to the special issue on school bullying. *School Psychology Review, 32*, 456–470.
Furst, Edward (1958). *Constructing evaluation instruments*. New York: David McKay.
Garbarino, James (2004). Forward. In Espelage, Dorothy L. and Swearer, Susan M. (Eds.), *Bullying in American schools: A social-ecological perspective on prevention and intervention*. Mahwah, NJ: Lawrence Erlbaum Associates.er
Ghent, Emmanuel (1990). Masochism, submission, surrender. *Contemporary Psychoanalysis, 26*, 108–136.
Giannetti, C., and Sagarese, M. (2001). *Cliques: 8 steps to help your child survive the jungle*. New York: Broadway Books.
Gilbert, P. (1992). *Depression: The evolution of powerlessness*. Hove, UK: Lawrence Erlbaum Associates.
Goldberg, D., and Williams, P. (1991). *A users' guide to the general health questionnaire*. Windsor: NFER-Nelson.
Hanish, Laura D., Kochenderfer-Ladd, Becky, Fabes, Richard A., Martin, Carol Lynn, and Deening, Donna (2004). Bullying among young children: The influence of peers and teachers. In Espelage, Dorothy L. and Swearer, Susan M. (Eds.), *Bullying in American schools: A social-ecological perspective on prevention and intervention*. Mahwah, NJ: Lawrence Erlbaum Associates.
Hawker, David S., and Boulton, Michael J. (2001). Subtypes of peer harassment and their correlates: A social dominance perspective. In Juvonen, Jaana, and Graham, Sandra (Eds.), *Peer harassment in school: The plight of the vulnerable and victimized* (pp. 378–397). New York: The Guilford Press.
Hawley, P.H. (1999). The ontogenesis of social dominance: A strategy-based evolutionary perspective. *Developmental Review, 19*, 97–132.

Hodges, E.V.E., Malone, M.J., and Perry, D.G. (1997). Individual risk and social risk as interacting determinants of victimization in the peer group. *Developmental Psychology, 33*, 1032–1039.

Holt, Melissa K., and Keyes, Melissa A. (2004). Teachers' attitudes toward bullying. In Espelage, Dorothy L., and Swearer, Susan M. (Eds.), *Bullying in American schools: A social-ecological perspective on prevention and intervention*. Mahwah, NJ: Lawrence Erlbaum Associates.

Hoover, John H., and Oliver, Ronald (1996). *The bullying prevention handbook: A guide for principals, teachers, and counselors*. Bloomington, IN: National Educational Service.

Hoover, J.H., Oliver, R, and Hazler, R.J. (1992). Bullying: Perceptions of adolescent victims in the Midwestern USA. *School Psychology International, 13*, 5–16.

Horne, Arthur M., Orpinas, Pamela, Newman-Carlson, Dawn, and Bartolomucci, Christi L. (2004). Elementary school Bully Busters program: Understanding why children bully and what to do about it. In Espelage, Dorothy L. and Swearer, Susan M. (Eds.), *Bullying in American schools: A social-ecological perspective on prevention and intervention*. Mahwah, NJ: Lawrence Erlbaum Associates.

Jacob, Phillip (1957). *Changing values in college*. New York: Harper.

Jacobson, Ronald B. (2007a). School bullying and current educational practice: Re-Imagining theories of educational transformation. *Teachers College Record, 109*(8): 1931–1956.

Jacobson, Ronald B. (2007b). *Understanding, Desire and Narrated Subjectivity: A Philosophical Consideration of the Phenomenon of School Bullying*. Dissertation: University of Washington.

———(2009a). A place to stand: Intersubjectivity and the desire to dominate. *Studies in Philosophy and Education, 29*, 35–51.

———(2009b). Public spaces and moral education. *Journal of Research in Character Education, 7*(1): 63–75.

———(2010a). Narrating characters: The making of a school bully. *Interchange, 41* (3): 255–283.

———(2010b). On bullshit and bullying: Taking seriously those we educate. *Journal of Moral Education, 39* (4): 437–448.

———(2010c). Moral education and the academics of being human together. *Journal of Thought*, Spring-Summer, 43–53.

Janssen, Ian, Craig, Wendy, Boyce, William F., and Pickett, William (2004). Associations between overweight and obesity with bullying behaviors in school-aged children. *Pediatrics, 113*, 1187–1194.

Johnson, M., Munn, P., and Edwards, L. (1991). *Action against bullying: A support pack for schools*. Edinburgh: The Scottish Council for Educational Research.

Juvonen, Janna, and Graham, Sandra (Eds.) (2001). *Peer harassment in school: The plight of the vulnerable and victimized*. New York: The Guilford Press.

Kaltialo-Heino, R., Rimpela, M., Marttunen, M., Rimpela, A., and Ratenen, P. (1999). Bullying, depression and suicidal ideation in Finnish adolescents: school survey. *British Medical Journal, 319*, 348–350.

Kasen, Stephanie, Berenson, Kathy, Cohen, Patricia, and Johnson, Jeffrey G. (2004). The effects of school climate on changes iressive and other behaviors related to bullying. In Espelage, Dorothy L. and Swearer, Susan M. (Eds.), *Bullying in American schools: A social-ecological perspective on prevention and intervention*. Mahwah, NJ: Lawrence Erlbaum Associates.

Kaukiainen, Ari, Bjorkqvist, Kaj, Lagerspetz, Kirsti, Osterman, Karin, Salmivalli, Christina, Rothberg, Sari, and Ahlbom, Anne (1999). The relationships between social intelligence, empathy, and three types of aggression. *Aggressive Behavior, 25*, 81–89.

Kester, Kira, and Mann, Candiya (2008). *Bullying in Washington schools: Update 2008*. Social and Economic Sciences Research Center; Puget Sound Division.
Kochenderfer, B.J., and Ladd, G.W. (1996). Peer victimization: Cause or consequence of school maladjustment. *Child Development, 67*, 1305–1317.
Krathwohl, D., Bloom, B., and Masia, B. (1964). *Taxonomy of educational objectives: The classification of educational goals: Handbook II: Affective domain*. New York: David McKay.
Lakatos, Imre (1970). Falsification and the methodology of scientific research programmes. In I. Lakatos and A. Musgrave (Eds.), *Criticism and the growth of knowledge*. Cambridge: Cambridge University Press.
Long, Jeffrey D., and Pellegrini, Anthony D. (2003). Studying change in dominance and bullying with linear mixed models. *School Psychology Review, 32*, 401–417.
Maines, B., and Robinson, G. (1992). *Michael's story: the 'No Blame' approach*. Bristol: Lame Duck Publishing.
Malecki, Christine Kerres, and Demaray, Michelle Kilpatrick (2004). The role of social support in the lives of bullies, victims, and bully-victims. In Espelage, Dorothy L. and Swearer, Susan M. (Eds.), *Bullying in American schools: A social-ecological perspective on prevention and intervention*. Mahwah, NJ: Lawrence Erlbaum Associates.
McNay, Lois (1992). *Foucault & feminism: Power, gender and the self*. Boston: Northeastern University Press.
Milgram, S. (1992). *The individual in a social world: Essays and experiments*. Sabini, J. and Silver, M. (Eds.). New York: McGraw-Hill.
Miller, P., and Eisenberg, N. (1988). The relation of empathy to aggressive and externalizing/antisocial behavior. *Psychological bulletin, 103*, 324–344.
Naylor, Paul, and Cowie, Helen (1999). The effectiveness of peer support systems in challenging school bullying: The perspectives and experiences of teachers and pupils. *Journal of Adolescence, 22*, 467–452.
O'Connell, Paul, Pepler, Debra, and Craig, Wendy (1999). The effectiveness of peer support systems in challenging school bullying: the perspectives and experiences of teachers and pupils. *Journal of Adolescence, 22*, 437–452.
O'Connor, M., Foch, T., Todd, S., and Plomin, R (1980). A twin study of specific behavioral problems of socialization as viewed by parents. *Journal of Abnormal Child Psychology, 8*, 189–199.
O'Moore, M., and Kirkham, C. (2001). Self-esteem and its relationship to bullying behaviour. *Aggressive Behavior, 27*, 269–283.
Olweus, Dan (1993). *Bullying at school*. Malden, MA: Blackwell Publishing.
Paley, Vivian Gussin (1992). *You can't say you can't play*. Cambridge: Harvard University Press.
Pellegrini, A.D., and Bartini, M. (2001). Dominance in early adolescent boys: Affiliative and aggressive dimensions and possible functions. *Merrill-Palmer Quarterly, 47*, 142–163.
Pellegrini, Anthony D. (2001). Sampling instances of victimization in middle school: A methodological comparison. In J. Juvonen and S. Graham (Eds.), *Peer harassment in school: The plight of the vulnerable and victimized* (pp. 125–144). New York: The Guilford Press.
(2002). Bullying and victimization in middle school: A dominance relations perspective. *Educational Psychologist, 37*, 151–163.
Pellegrini, Anthony D., and Long, Jeffrey D. (2002). A longitudinal study of bullying, dominance, and victimization during the transition from primary to secondary school. *British Journal of Developmental Psychology, 20*, 259–280.

———(2003). A sexual selection theory longitudinal analysis of sexual segregation and integration in early adolescence. *Journal of Experimental Child Psychology, 85,* 257–278.

———(2004). Part of the solution and part of the problem: The role of peers in bullying, dominance, and victimization during the transition from primary school through secondary school. In Espelage, Dorothy L. and Swearer, Susan M. (Eds.), *Bullying in American schools: A social-ecological perspective on prevention and intervention.* Mahwah, NJ: Lawrence Erlbaum Associates.

Pepler, D., and Craig, W. (1995). A peek behind the fence: Naturalistic observations of aggressive children with remote audiovisual recording. *Developmental Psychology, 31,* 548–553.

Perry, David G., Hodges, Ernest V.E., and Egan, Susan K. (2001). Determinants of chronic victimization by peers: A review and a new model of family influence. In Juvonen, Jaana, and Graham, Sandra (Eds.), *Peer harassment in school: The plight of the vulnerable and victimized* (pp. 49–72). New York: The Guilford Press.

Phillips, Adam (2002). *Equals.* New York: Basic Books.

Phillips, Deborah (2000). *Exploring new directions for ending practices of male violence: Masculinity, adolescent boys, and culture.* Ph.D. dissertation, University of Washington.

Prinstein, M.J., and Cohen, G.L. (2001, April). *Adolescent peer crowd affiliation and overt, relational, and social aggression: Using aggression to protect one's peer status.* Paper presented at the biennial meeting of the Society for Research in Child Development, Minneapolis, MN.

Rigby, K., Cox, I.K., and Black, G. (1997). Cooperativeness and bully/victim problems among Australian schoolchildren. *Journal of Social Psychology, 137,* 3, 357–368.

Rigby, K., and Slee, P.T. (1999). Suicidal ideation among adolescent school children, involvement in bully/victim problems and perceived low social support. *Suicide and Life-threatening Behavior, 29,* 119–130.

Rigby, Ken (2002). *New perspectives on bullying.* London: Jessica Kingsley Publishers.

(1997a). *Manual for the peer relations questionnaire (PRQ).* Point Lonsdale, Victoria, Australia: The Professional Reading Guide.

(1997b). *Manual for the Peer Relations Questionnaire (PRQ).* Point Lonsdale, Victoria, Austrialia: The Professional Reading Guide.

Rodkin, Philip C. (2004). Peer ecologies of aggression and bullying. In Espelage, Dorothy L. and Swearer, Susan M. (Eds.), *Bullying in American schools: A social-ecological perspective on prevention and intervention.* Mahwah, NJ: Lawrence Erlbaum Associates.

Roland, E. (1989). A system-oriented strategy against bullying. In Roland, E. and Muthe, E. (Eds.), *Bullying: An international perspective.* London: Professional Development Foundation.

Salmivalli, C., Lagerspetz, K., Bjuorkqvist, K., Osterman, K., and Kaukiainen, A. (1996). Bullying as a group process: Participant roles and their relations to social status within the group. *Aggressive Behavior, 22,* 1–15.

Salmivalli, Christina (1999). Participant role approach to school bullying: Implications for interventions. *Journal of Adolescence, 22,* 453–459.

Salmivalli, Christina and Nieminen, Eija (2002). Proactive and reactive aggression among school bullies, victims, and bully-victims. *Aggressive Behavior, 28,* 30–44.

Schwartz, David, Proctor, Laura J., and Chien, Deborah H. (2001). The aggressive victim of bullying: Emotional and behavioral disregulation as a pathway to victimization by peers. In Juvonen, Jaana, and Graham, Sandra (Eds.), *Peer harassment in school: The plight of the vulnerable and victimized* (pp. 49–72). New York: The Guilford Press.

Scuster, Beate (2001). Rejection and victimization by peers: Social perception and social behavior mechanisms. In Juvonen, Jaana, and Graham, Sandra (Eds.), *Peer harassment in school: The plight of the vulnerable and victimized* (pp. 49–72). New York: The Guilford Press.

Sheridan, Susan M., Warnes, Emily D., and Dowd, Shannon (2004). Home-school collaboration and bullying: An ecological approach to increase social competence in children and youth. In Espelage, Dorothy L. and Swearer, Susan M. (Eds.), *Bullying in American schools: A social-ecological perspective on prevention and intervention*. Mahwah, NJ: Lawrence Erlbaum Associates.

Simmons, Rachel (2002). *Odd girl out: The hidden culture of aggression in girls*. New York: Harcourt.

Smith, Christian (2003). *Moral, believing animals: Human personhood and culture*. New York,: Oxford University Press.

Smith, Peter K., Shu, Shu, and Madsen, Kirsten (2001). Characteristics of victims of school bullying: Developmental changes in coping strategies and skills. In Juvonen, Jaana, and Graham, Sandra (Eds.), *Peer harassment in school: The plight of the vulnerable and victimized* (pp. 49–72). New York: The Guilford Press.

Strayer, F.F. (1980). Social ecology of the preschool peer group. In W.A. Collins (Ed.), *The Minnesota symposia on child psychology. Development of cognition, affect, and social relations, 13*, 165–196. Hillsdale, NJ: Lawrence Erlbaum Associates.

Sutton, J., and Smith, P.K. (1999). Bullying as a group process: An adaptation of the participant role approach. *Aggressive Behavior, 25*, 97–111.

Sutton, J., Smith, P.K., and Swettenham, J. (1999). Socially undesirable need not be incompetent: A response to Crick and Dodge. *Social Development, 8*, 132–134.

Swearer, Susan M., Grills, Amie E., Haye, Kisha M., and Cary, Paulette Tam (2004). Internalizing problems in students involved in bullying and victimization: Implications for intervention. In Espelage, Dorothy L. and Swearer, Susan M. (Eds.), *Bullying in American schools: A social-ecological perspective on prevention and intervention*. Mahwah, NJ: Lawrence Erlbaum Associates.

Tyler, Ralph (1934). *Constructing achievement tests*. Columbus, OH: Ohio State University Press.

Vaernes, R.J., Myhre, G.A., Henrik, H., and Homnes, T. (1991). Work and stress: Relationships between stress, psychological factors and immune levels among military aviators. *Work and Stress, 5*, 5–16.

Whitaker D.J., Rosenbluth, B., L.A., Valle, and Sanchez, E. (2004). Expect respect: A school-based intervention to promote awareness and effective responses to bullying and sexual harassment. In Espelage, Dorothy L. and Swearer, Susan M. (Eds.), *Bullying in American schools: A social-ecological perspective on prevention and intervention*. Mahwah, NJ: Lawrence Erlbaum Associates.

Index

A
Anti-Bullying Strategies, 41–43

B
Bloom & Krathwohl, 83, 88–95
Bully Busters, 41
Bullying
   Prevalence, 11–12, 15–16
   Characteristics of a bully, 18–23
   Characteristics of a victim, 23–26
   Definition, 12–14
   Effects of, 16–18
   Gender, 31–34
   Motivations, 34–39
   Roles in the bullying dynamic, 29–30

C
Common Concern Method, 41

D
Dewey, 79–83, 88, 95, 98, 134
Dividing practices, 64–69, 71–72

E
Espelage, 11, 12, 17, 19–20, 22, 32, 34–35, 37–39, 44
Expect Respect, 41, 125–127

L
Lakatos, 85–88, 98, 134
Long, 13, 21, 27, 28, 37, 45–46, 58, 144

O
Object Destruction, 55–56
Object Usage, 53–57
Olweus, 11–16, 20–24, 28, 31, 35–39, 41–42, 125

P
Paley, 95–101, 134
Pellegrini, 13, 21, 27, 28, 37, 45–46, 58, 144
Preferred image, 48, 50–51

R
Rigby, 15–17, 19, 28, 32, 35, 37–39

S
Salmivalli, 13–14, 21, 30
Simmons, 11, 14, 16, 25, 31–34, 36, 63
Status, 57–59, 61, 71
Strategic teams, 138–139
Strategy building questions, 135–138
Steps to Respect, 41
Swearer, 11, 12, 14, 19–20, 22, 32, 35–39, 44